Great Power Interests in the Persian Gulf

§

Great Power Interests
in the Persian Gulf

§

Paul Jabber

Gary Sick

Hisahiko Okazaki

Dominique Moîsi

Council on Foreign Relations

New York

COUNCIL ON FOREIGN RELATIONS BOOKS

Library of Congress Cataloging-in-Publication Data

Great power interests in the Persian Gulf / Paul Jabber . . . [et al.].
    p.   cm.
    ISBN 0-87609-046-3
    1. Persian Gulf Region--Politics and government. 2. United States--Foreign relations--Persian Gulf Region. 3. Persian Gulf Region--Foreign relations--United States. I. Jabber, Paul, 1943-
. II. Council on Foreign Relations.
DS326.G67 1988   88-39443
                                          CIP

Contents

Foreword

It has become increasingly important that Americans understand the strategic importance of the Persian Gulf states and Pakistan because of Western dependence on oil in a region so close to the Soviet Union. The bitter, long war between Iran and Iraq clearly underscored this need. Accordingly, the Arthur Ross Foundation agreed to sponsor a program that was organized by the Council on Foreign Relations in 1987/88 to invite a number of distinguished speakers and to convene a study group on great power interests and policies in the area.

The Council undertook a series of seven meetings that featured the Foreign Ministers of Pakistan, Egypt and Iraq, the Minister of Petroleum and Mineral Resources from Saudi Arabia, Frank Carlucci, who was then National Security Advisor to the President, Amin Saikal on the Soviet dilemma in Afghanistan, and General Crist who was Commander-in-Chief of the U.S. Central Command.

These were followed in March by a one-session study group convened in New York under the chairmanship of James R. Schlesinger, former Secretary of Energy and Defense as well as Director of the CIA. The group, which included many of the nation's leading authorities on the subject, conducted its discussion on the basis of papers and comments from: Gary Sick, formerly with the National Security Council and the Ford Foundation, giving an American perspective, Ambassador Hisahiko Okazaki, giving a Japanese perspective, and Dominique Moîsi of the French Institute of International Relations, giving a European perspective. The Council also arranged participation for part of the session by observers from the Soviet and Chinese Missions to the United Nations as well as from the United Nations Secretariat.

This book does not pretend to be a comprehensive survey of all aspects of the Gulf problem. More modestly, it is a collection of papers by highly qualified authors deliberately selected to reflect a range of views on a region of critical importance to the West and Japan. Three of the essays in this volume are the papers commissioned for the study group. The fourth is an introductory essay by Paul Jabber, until recently the Council's Senior Fellow for the Middle East. Although written before the authors saw any signs that Iran and Iraq were prepared to accept a cease-fire, the three discussion papers anticipated that event as inevitable. Together with Paul Jabber's essay it is hoped that the material will be found instructive. The Foundation was indeed pleased to support this Council project.

Arthur Ross
President
Arthur Ross Foundation

August 1988

Introduction: Western Interests and Gulf Stability

Paul Jabber

The interests of the West and Japan in the Persian Gulf area are both unambiguous and vital. For much of the 1980s, these interests have also been clearly at risk. They revolve mainly around the critical issue of energy security, as they have for some four decades. The region is by far the largest remaining world source of cheap hydrocarbons in a global economy that continues to be oil-based. By one authoritative estimate, as of the end of 1987, proven crude oil reserves of the gulf countries amounted to 70 percent (565 billion barrels) of total reserves available worldwide outside the Communist bloc. The gulf currently exports about ten million barrels per day, a quarter of total world consumption.

A complementary geostrategic interest stems from the proximity of the U.S.S.R to this area. Moscow's historic ambitions for expansion to the south prompted the leadership of the Western Alliance early in the postwar period to identify a serious Soviet threat to Western interests in the Middle East. It should be recalled that one of the opening moves in the cold war was Stalin's attempt in 1945-1946 to set up a satellite Azerbaijani state in northern Iran. The invasion of Afghanistan in 1979 brought Soviet military installations to within easy striking distance of the Arabian Sea. Recognition of the region's strategic value led the United States in 1949 to establish a permanent naval presence in the gulf, based in Bahrain. It also underlies the most recent buildup of U.S. and Western forces in the gulf and Arabian Sea, which by the fall

1

of 1987 consisted of more than sixty naval units, thirty of them American, including two carrier task forces.

The crux of the matter is that it is in the vital military and economic interest of both the United States and the Western Alliance to maintain unfettered access to the world's largest oil reserves at reasonable, acceptable prices. This point was amply demonstrated in 1973 and 1979 when relatively minor disruptions to the oil supply caused by events in the Middle East enabled the Organization of Petroleum Exporting Countries (OPEC) to engineer rapid and drastic rises in oil prices, with major disruptive effects on the global economy. Moreover, this dependence is likely to exist for at least the next two decades. Indeed, all indications are that reliance on gulf oil by the industrial world will grow in the decade ahead and will not peak before the next century.

How is this vital national interest to be secured? In practice, it can be done only through the preservation of a regional system in the gulf that safeguards the ability of the various local countries to set their own policies freely. The problem is not simply the availability of gulf oil to the world. By necessity, the gulf countries have to sell their only major exportable commodity. What is at issue is the price at which oil will be made available in an increasingly oligopolistic setting. In other words, the emergence of any hegemonic power in the gulf—whether local or external to the region— capable of substantially directing, let alone controlling outright, the oil production and pricing policies of the key producing states (Saudi Arabia, Kuwait, Iran, Iraq, Qatar, and the UAE) could be disastrous for the West.

More manageable for the industrial economies but still a significant threat is the possibility of a Gulf "mini-OPEC" emerging in the mid-1990's. Consisting of the largest exporters, who already make up the core power bloc within the organization, such a grouping could prove to be a more cohesive and effective cartel in the much tighter market conditions likely to prevail toward the end of the century. A Gulf OPEC would control most of the world's cheap oil reserves, and might include only surplus producers, i.e.

countries whose relatively small populations and healthy
financial status would afford them more leeway in the
manipulation of oil pricing/production levels. Fortunately, as
Gulf producers continue to increase their direct investments
in tho OECD countrioc, thoy may coo that it io no longor in
their interest to behave in ways that might cause major
imbalances in the world economy. Particularly significant is
their growing stake in the downstream energy sector, pio-
neered by Kuwait's acquisition of refineries and a retail
marketing network in Western Europe, and a similar joint
venture in the United States between Saudi Arabia and
Texaco announced in July 1988. Such investments provide
these oil-producing countries with guaranteed outlets for
their crude exports and a strong competitive incentive to
maintain price stability.

External Threats: The Soviet Union

From the West's perspective, the only meaningful external
hegemonic threat is posed by the Soviet Union. A Soviet
attack southward is an ever-present contingency that military
planners must worry about, but one that rates a very low
probability under present conditions, particularly in light of
Moscow's bitter experience in Afghanistan which proved
particularly costly to the Soviets throughout the Middle East.

The advance of Soviet political influence presents a more
immediate challenge. Across the whole range of Middle East
issues, the Soviet Union traditionally has ranged itself in
opposition to the West and its regional friends. What might
have been termed a "normal" cold war dynamic based on
standard balance-of-power considerations was given further
impetus by the heavy projection of Western military power
into the area since mid-1987. Paradoxically, however, Moscow's reluctance to confront Teheran, insofar as it helped
prolong the war, also promoted those conditions that justified
the introduction of large-scale Western military forces.

Nevertheless, the Middle East has witnessed several in-
stances of substantial improvements in the Soviet position

over the past two years, as a result of the renewed vigor and flexibility exhibited by Moscow in its regional policies under Mikhail Gorbachev. In the gulf, diplomatic ties have been established with Oman, the United Arab Emirates and Qatar. A more active dialogue with Saudi Arabia has resulted in repeated consultations over oil policy and bilateral high-level visits. The estrangement with Egypt has ended, and a rescheduling of long-standing military debt on very favorable terms has opened the way for broader trade relations and encouraged Cairo to assume a more "balanced" posture toward the two superpowers. Perhaps most significant in this respect are Moscow's various efforts to position itself for an active role in Arab-Israeli peace diplomacy, including steps to improve relations with Israel, both on a bilateral basis and in the sensitive context of Jewish emigration.

Despite its new nimbleness and pragmatism, however, the Soviet Union is likely to continue to face severe handicaps in any attempt to gain predominant influence in the Middle East. As with other major external powers, it is hobbled by the suspicion and hostility of native political forces, which remain fiercely nationalistic, and in many cases have become further imbued in recent years with the xenophobia of militant Islam. In addition, it is incapable of offering competitive inducements, such as high technology, financing, consumer products, or access to attractive investment markets, that might prompt local partners to offer it favored status.

Regional Threats: Iran

Since the late 1970's, a far more immediate threat to Western interests than Soviet ambitions has emanated from within the region, following the coming to power in Iran of the Islamic revolutionary regime headed by the Ayatollah Rouhollah Khomeini. This threat stemmed partly from the ideological underpinnings of the new regime and partly from its posture and objectives in the war with Iraq, which, at face value, were tantamount to an effort to impose Iranian hegemony over the region.

Had the war ended in victory for the Khomeini regime, the results could have been nothing short of catastrophic for the interests of the West and the stability of the Middle East. A triumphant Iran would have given great momentum to religious fundamentalism in many parts of the Islamic world and severely threatened the survival of friendly governments in the decade ahead. Saudi Arabia and the smaller gulf states could have been so intimidated in the face of Iranian regional supremacy that Teheran would have been able to impose itself on their oil production and pricing policies. Iran would have become the master of OPEC.

Iran's sudden announcement on July 18, 1988, of its decision to accept "unconditionally" the call for a cease-fire under United Nations Security Council Resolution 598 opened the way for the shaky truce that exists today. For its part, Iraq accepted this international edict shortly after its adoption in July 1987. A negotiated outcome that leaves both contending regimes and their territories intact would be welcomed as the least destabilizing for the whole region. While the prospect of upheaval by military force that has haunted the countries of the gulf area seems at last on the point of dissipating, the future course of Iran's relations both with its Arab neighbors and the West remains quite uncertain.

Mainsprings and Implications of Iran's Policy

Iran has been a major—and often stabilizing—influence in the region for much of the past four decades. But the policies of the current leadership have been fueled by an explosive mixture: historical objectives that come from the country's ample geopolitical and demographic attributes, and the messianic impulse of a revolutionary Islamic fundamentalist ideology.

Iran's traditional aspirations to regional supremacy have in the past been kept in check by a rough balance of power with Iraq, the latter being buttressed by the implicit support of its Arab brethren in any conflict pitting Arabs against Persians. In any case, even at the height of its military strength in the

1970s, Iran under the Shah was content with exercising the role of the "Guardian of the Gulf" in a manner that was generally protective of the political status quo.

Although Iran flexed its muscles with impunity in a clear demonstration of its supremacy when it occupied the disputed Abu Musa and Tunbs islands in the lower gulf in November 1971, the Shah generally avoided direct confrontation with his neighbors. In 1970 he renounced all claims to Bahrain and in 1975 signed a treaty that settled boundary disputes with Iraq. Iran's interest in the stability of conservative rule within the Arabian peninsula states was further demonstrated by its active role in helping the Sultan of Oman defeat the insurgency led by the Marxist PFLOAG (Popular Front for the Liberation of the Occupied Arab Gulf with the backing of South Yemen in the early 1970s.

The dynamics of the regional system changed drastically in 1979. A clerical leadership emerged from the ashes of the coalition that overthrew the Shah in 1978 to become the sole master of Iran. Shi'a fundamentalist in its ideology, radically subversive and aggressively unconventional in its methods, as well as militantly transnational in both its appeal and its program, the Islamic Republic of Iran became a powerful motor—and blueprint—for revolutionary change and a threat by definition to every other political system in the region.

Teheran's hostility toward the Saudis and other gulf regimes is not simply a temporary by-product of the war with Iraq. Its long-term goal has been actively to promote conditions both region-wide and within each country that will help bring about new governments faithful to the path of Islamic justice as defined by Teheran. This is an ideological purpose born of the self-image and convictions of the top leadership. The fact that most of the gulf states have either Shi'a majorities or very sizable Shi'a minorities, and that they all are governed by Sunnis who have often discriminated against their Shi'a citizens, albeit in varying degrees, added a powerful sectarian dimension to the confrontation. Furthermore, it provided a neat cognitive fit with the worldview of the Ayatollah Khomeini and his followers, which emphasizes the irreconcilable differences between the oppressors and the oppressed.

Events since the birth of the Islamic Republic, particularly the Iran-Iraq war, have tended to widen the ethnic divisions between Arabs and Persians while reinforcing the bonds of nationalist loyalty. This was apparent in the performance of Iraq's Shi'a majority, which provided the bulk of Iraq's fighting forces and remained loyal to the government of President Saddam Hussein, himself a Sunni. It was also evident in the behavior of Iran's regular armed forces and many elements of its technocratic and commercial elites, who may not have supported clerical rule, but saw the war as a justified effort of self-defense against Arab territorial designs on Khuzistan.

Until very recently, the Teheran government seemed determined not to accept a draw in this war. Behind its insistence on the demise of the Iraqi leadership, to be followed by heavy reparations payments, and its expectation that a radically different system of government was bound to emerge in Baghdad, lay a complex of motives. They prominently included: revenge; a conviction on the part of Khomeini and his followers that they are instruments of God's will; fear of the consequences for the regime of a failure to redeem with victory the vast sacrifices imposed by the war effort; and the resolve of Iranian nationalists to seize the opportunity to establish Iran firmly as the region's controlling power.

This determination remained unshakable as long as Iran retained the ability to mount a significant level of military pressure. Over the past two years evidence began to mount that, even with periodic reaffirmation by the Imam himself of the holy necessity of the struggle, Teheran was finding it increasingly hard to marshall the requisite level of effort from an exhausted population facing an increasingly difficult set of external challenges. The collapse of international oil prices in late 1985 and 1986 was a particularly devastating blow, given Iran's exclusive reliance on oil-export revenues to finance itself. On the other hand, it also became evident that, unless the regime's war-making capability was crippled in its finances and its weapons procurement, the conflict would continue. The strong Iranian assault on the approaches to Iraq's second largest city, Basra, at the end of 1986 gave renewed evidence of the mullahs' determination.

Last Stages Of A Stalemated War

But Basra did not fall, and the war settled back into its fitful stalemated condition. Over the past year, perhaps the key development was literally a nonevent: Iran's failure at the end of 1987 to launch its annual major winter offensive on the southern front. Instead, the Iranians announced a new strategy of smaller and more frequent offensives along the entire length of the border with Iraq. The most important of these took place in the north, where Iraqi Kurdish rebel forces allied with Teheran helped the revolutionary guards occupy a number of Iraqi villages following a penetration of some ten to fifteen miles into Iraq in the direction of Suleymaniyyah. But the northern front was not where Iran could win this war. Its advances in this area were limited by difficult mountainous terrain, and the key strategic prize in the region, the Kirkuk oil fields and the pipeline that carries Iraqi oil exports through Turkey to Mediterranean outlets, remained some sixty miles to the west.

Iraq responded with stepped up efforts to force Iran to accept the cease-fire terms of U.N. Resolution 598 by carrying the war to Iranian population centers and making repeated strikes against economic targets. Frequent air and long-range missile raids on Teheran and other major cities were unleashed, provoking similar retaliatory strikes by the Iranians. Sporadically, the Iraqi air force also continued to strike at oil tankers and other shipping in and out of the Iranian ports in the gulf, as well as Iranian oil-loading facilities.

The routine use of ballistic missiles against population centers and the repeated resort to chemical warfare on the frontlines were among the most notable features of the war in its latter stages. These are ominous developments in a region such as the Middle East, where unresolved international conflicts are rife and nuclear proliferation looms in the background as a next stage in the regional arms race.

With the passage of U.N. Resolution 598 (see text in the Appendix) in July 1987, the continuing military stalemate focused attention on diplomatic efforts to end the fighting. For almost a full year, diplomacy was frustrated by Teheran's refusal to abide by the terms of the Resolution. To further constrain Iran's dwindling capacity to sustain the war effort or seriously threaten the security of the smaller gulf states, the Reagan administration strongly supported the imposition of an arms embargo against Iran as a sanction for its refusal to accept the U.N. mandated cease-fire. Although supported by the European allies, such sanctions ran into Soviet opposition. Also opposed to an arms embargo was the People's Republic of China, which has emerged in recent years as Iran's single largest source of imported weaponry.

The Soviet discomfort was understandable, given the mullahs' ability to fan the flames of fundamentalist Islamic unrest in Soviet Central Asia. Recent clashes between Christian Armenians and Muslim Azerbaijanis are painful reminders for the Soviet leadership of the potential explosiveness of ethnic and religious issues in their southern republics. Also, Iran's extensive borders with the Soviet Union, its size, location, and resources are obvious incentives for Moscow to keep its relations with Teheran from deteriorating into confrontation. Besides, the Soviets can continue to exploit U.S.-Iranian antagonism to their own advantage.

The sequence of events that appears to have persuaded the Iranian leadership that it courted disaster unless the fighting stopped began in April 1988, with the retaking of the Fao peninsula by Iraqi forces. Accomplished quickly and without significant losses, this campaign by a revitalized Iraqi army was followed in subsequent weeks by several thrusts along the southern and northern fronts. These actions wrested from the Iranians practically all Iraqi border areas that Iran had succeeded in conquering at great cost in repeated human-wave offensives since 1982. Coupled with the manifest inability of Iranian air defenses to protect Teheran from widespread damage and dislocation of its inhabitants inflicted by Iraq's air and missile strikes from February to April, this series of battlefield setbacks was devastating to Iranian morale.

A critical turning point leading to Khomeini's acceptance of U.N. Resolution 598 on July 18 may have been the capture by Iraq on July 13 of Dehloran, a town lying near a strategic crossroads, some twenty miles inside Iranian territory. That Iraqi forces could now strike successfully into Iran proper threatened to place Iran's leadership in the politically intolerable position of having to accede to a cease-fire with some of its own territory in Iraqi hands. Suddenly, for Iran in the summer of 1988, an early cease-fire had become perhaps the only way to snatch a face-saving draw from the jaws of impending defeat.

Risks and Opportunities for the United States

From an American perspective, an early end to the gulf conflict should be particularly welcome. Without a stable cease-fire, followed by an active process of political settlement of issues dividing Iran and Iraq, the likelihood of deeper entanglement by the United States in the region remains high.

Iran's prominence as a regional power, its status as one of the largest oil-reserve countries, and its value as a market for U.S. goods argue for the earliest possible normalization of ties. Yet the obstacles to speedy normalization will be great, even in a post-war environment. Among the most important are the traumatic record of U.S.-Iranian relations since the 1978 revolution; strong domestic political and ideological rivalries in Iran, further complicated by the ongoing struggle over the succession to the ailing Khomeini; the political inhibitions in the United States against any dealings with Teheran that might smack of "Irangate"—the failed and highly unpopular effort by the Reagan White House in 1985-1986 secretly to supply arms to Iran in exchange for release of Americans held hostage in Lebanon; and Iran's highly unorthodox, if not outright subversive, behavior and policies toward several key friends of the United States in the Middle East.

While improvement in U.S.-Iran ties will be a slow and difficult process, the current situation does present opportunities for American policy toward other countries in the region. Despite initial forebodings, the heavy U.S. buildup, with its requirements for access to local facilities of Arab gulf states, close cooperation with the military establishments of these countries, and a higher profile for U.S. forces overall, was increasingly accepted (in some cases even welcomed) in key gulf capitals. The U.S. military buildup also received at least a temporary seal of approval from Baghdad, which since the 1958 overthrow of the monarchy had been resolutely opposed on Arab nationalist grounds to an enhanced Western presence in the area.

Two events in particular have helped trigger this evolution in Arab gulf attitudes. One was Kuwait's taking the initiative in requesting external intervention—a critical ingredient in legitimizing the U.S. role. The other was the Mecca incidents on July 31, 1987, at the height of the annual Islamic pilgrimage, when several hundred militant Iranians and many Saudis died in riots caused by an apparent Iranian plot to forcibly occupy the Kaaba, Islam's holiest shrine. These events, which were the culmination of two years of sustained Iranian effort to intimidate Kuwait and Saudi Arabia into withdrawing their financial and political backing for Iraq, appear to have crystallized for the GCC (Gulf Cooperation Council) countries the magnitude of the threat they face from Iran.

With the growing support of several NATO allies, including the deployment of a French carrier task force, and British, Dutch, Belgian, and Italian units, U.S. forces by early 1988 had drawn a red line protecting the vulnerable sheikhdoms on the Arab side of the gulf, as well as Saudi Arabia, from Iranian encroachment. Mainly as a result of this decisive and sustained action by Washington, U.S.-Arab relations in this critical area of the Middle East are today on a sounder footing than at any time since the 1950s.

With the "Irangate" affair still fresh in the minds of all concerned, it should be emphasized that this attitudinal shift is still in its formative stage and remains highly dependent on U.S. steadfastness and consistency in its policies toward the region. In particular, care should be taken that a future rapprochement with Iran does not undo the progress achieved in the recent past, whether in matters of security cooperation with the GCC states, or political relations with an Iraq that in recent years has clearly reoriented its foreign policy towards cooperation with the West and is striving to liberalize its economy.

The evolution of U.S.-Iraqi ties in the post-war era will in part be determined by the way in which Baghdad manages its relations with the gulf states. An aggressive pursuit of claims to regional leadership—as experienced in the 1970s—would cause great discomfort in Saudi Arabia, Kuwait and other countries, particularly if accomplished by a revival of territorial claims on Kuwait. Strong friction may arise over oil production policies as well, were Iraq to remain unwilling to abide by restrictive OPEC quotas while steadily increasing its exports. Relations with Washington would also be subject to severe strains were Iraq to adopt a confrontational stance vis-à-vis Israel, particularly in view of its new status as a major battle-tested regional power. On the other hand, the growing economic ties between the two countries—Iraq is today the third largest Middle East market for U.S. goods, and the second largest world recipient of U.S. agricultural credits—and the fact that Iraqi regional ambitions will necessarily remain constricted for the foreseeable future by the presence of an essentially hostile Iran on its borders, are important factors that work in favor of at least reasonably good relations with the United States.

A discordant note is periodically sounded in U.S Congressional debate over the sale of advanced U.S. military technology to Saudi Arabia and other Arab gulf states, driven by congressional concerns over the impact of such sales on Israeli security. This is a self-defeating exercise. The net effect of such congressional opposition has been to reorient the procurement efforts of these countries in the direction of Western Europe, China, and other ready suppliers. Quite apart from the loss of some $35 billion in U.S. export revenues during this decade alone, the illogic of this posture from the standpoint of Israeli security concerns is underlined by the fact that the U.S. military equipment is always sold under far more restrictive conditions attending its use, deployment, and third-party transfers than required by any other weapons supplier.

Finally, American policy in the gulf area must be framed within the broader context of U.S. Middle East policy, particularly in a postwar setting where the immediate security threat to the stability of the oil-producing Arab states will have diminished, and with it the pressing need for a substantial American military presence. At this broader regional level, the impact of the still unresolved Arab-Israeli conflict remains paramount. It is no secret that strong and consistent American support for Israel since the foundation of the Jewish state has been a key impediment to close and stable security relations between the United States and the Arab world. Nowhere does this hold more true than in the gulf states, where large and influential Palestinian communities reside.

If both of these policy concerns are to be pursued in tandem, only a continuous, high-level commitment by the U.S. government to peace diplomacy can alleviate the inherent tension between them. A decade ago, the Camp David process was a key breakthrough, making possible substantial political and military ties with Egypt. In the recent past, after a long and unfortunate hiatus, the efforts of Secretary of State George Shultz to break the current deadlock are a step in the right direction even if they prove unsuccessful. Ultimately, the fate of any international peace initiative rests in the hands of the local parties. Nonetheless, the simple act of persistent diplomatic engagement yields beneficial side effects in bilateral relations region-wide and provides an essential backstop to evolving security and political relationships with friendly states in the gulf and elsewhere in the Middle East that are likely to be vital to the safeguard of Western strategic and economic interests for the balance of this century and beyond.

In the contributions that follow, three distinguished observers of the gulf crisis provide perspectives on the major issues raised by eight years of continuing hostilities between Iran and Iraq. The papers were written for a Council Discussion Group that was convened prior to any convincing signs that the Iran-Iraq war might be drawing to a close. Gary Sick follows a historical approach, analyzing U.S. policies toward the area as they have evolved since World War II to illustrate his central contention that, notwithstanding a clear vision of their national interests, great powers have had great difficulty translating vision into policy. Particularly in a region as fraught with intractable local conflicts and conflicting external influences as the Middle East, he cautions, great powers have very limited control over events, and their interests are best protected if they are in congruence with those of relevant regional states.

Japan's policy toward the war has been shaped by its heavy dependence on gulf oil and its unwillingness to jeopardize friendly relations with any major producer by taking sides in political disputes, avers Hisahiko Okazaki, Tokyo's former ambassador to Saudi Arabia. He counsels restraint in Western efforts to influence Teheran so as to avoid giving Moscow opportunities to expand Soviet influence, while applauding the U.S. show-of-force as a necessary deterrent.

For Dominique Moisi, there is no "European" perspective on the gulf, or a common policy, but a set of rather distinct national policies that, in the case of the two most important European powers in the region, Great Britain and France, are reflective of their historical involvement in the area. He perceives British policy as tilting toward Iran, while France's sympathies are clearly with Iraq. He also underlines the dangers that Islamic fundamentalism poses for French relations with the Maghreb countries, and even for social peace within France itself, where upward of two million Moslems dwell. After initial skepticism, the new American role in the gulf is viewed positively in Europe, but the internationalization of the conflict also has given the Soviets a larger role in a region where their presence had been previously marginal.

In the text of the papers presented for discussion as well as in the course of the Council group's deliberations, the participants wrestled with two key policy dilemmas and shared one note of relief. The dilemmas were (a) how to move the diplomatic process forward in face of Iran's rejection of the Security Council's unanimously adopted Resolution 598, and of the unwillingness of key Council members to impose sanctions; and (b) how to contain Teheran—at times necessarily through the use of defensive or retaliatory military force—without pushing its leadership into Moscow's arms. The one comforting fact was the ability of the international oil markets to sustain reasonably low prices for most of the 1980s despite the damage inflicted on gulf oil facilities and the vicissitudes of the tanker war.

As this volume goes to print, the onset of negotiations between Iran and Iraq at United Nations headquarters over the terms of a cease-fire warrants a more optimistic note, now that eight years of bitter warfare may be drawing to a close. As peace returns to the gulf region, it is also to be hoped that a more predictable environment will translate into more stable oil prices, to the benefit of both supplier and consumer nations.

August 1988

An American Perspective

Gary Sick

This paper was prepared for presentation at a March 1988 Study Group. It has not been revised to reflect the cease-fire that has taken effect in the Persian Gulf war.

It is tempting to regard the policy of a great power simply as the derivative of its national interests. At some abstract level, that is true or perhaps a truism but it implies a degree of inevitability seldom present in the policy process. The texture of any country's policy is revealed in the uncertainties, misapprehensions, false starts, and tergiversations that are characteristic of thoroughly human policymakers as they try to cope with the unexpected twists and turns of circumstances largely beyond their control. A nation's interests may indeed be permanent and immutable, but whether and how to pursue those interests is a function of choice, hence fallible.

Analysis of the interactions between interests and policy must begin with consideration of several prior questions.: How did policymakers acquire their perception of interests? Have their perceptions changed over time or with new leadership? How have national leaders attempted to translate their understanding of interests into concrete policies? Have those policies changed in the face of new circumstances? Are the interests of the great power congruent with or contrary to the interests of the regional states? Have the policies of the great power succeeded in preserving and furthering its interests?

The interests of the United States in the Persian Gulf region have been very simple and consistent: first, to ensure access by the industrialized world to the vast oil resources of the region; and second, to prevent the Soviet Union from acquiring political or military control over those resources. Other objectives have been expressed by U.S. leaders from time to time; for example, preserving the stability and independence of the Gulf states or containing the threat of Islamic fundamentalism. But those are derivative concerns growing out of specific circumstances and are implicit in the two grand themes of oil and Soviet containment that have been the constant elements in U.S. policy.

The British Legacy

U.S. position in the Persian Gulf is descended lineally from the British, who dominated the region for nearly 150 years before the arrival of Americans.[1] The United States inherited not only its mantle of leadership and much of its strategic infrastructure from the British but also its way of thinking about its interests and how to pursue them.

The U.S. preoccupation with preventing the expansion of Soviet influence in the region can be seen as an extension of "The Great Game" that the British practiced throughout the nineteenth century. The other major concern of U.S. policy— how to ensure access to the oil resources of the region—is in turn reminiscent of British protection of its markets and lines of communication East of Suez. Thus, at least partly as a consequence of this historical evolution, there is a line of continuity in U.S policy and its perception of national interests in the Persian Gulf region that transcends any administration or political philosophy.[2]

United States interest and involvement in the Persian Gulf began in World War II, when the region became an important supply route for delivery of lend-lease military equipment and other supplies to the Soviet Union. At the beginning of the war, the British and Soviets deposed Reza Shah, placed his son on the throne, and effectively divided Iran between them. The 40,000 troops of the U.S. Middle East Command during those days still represent the largest sustained deployment of U.S. military personnel to the region.

The Teheran Conference in 1943 was the first visit by an American president to the region, and President Franklin Roosevelt's encounter with the young Mohammed Reza Shah Pahlavi sparked the first high-level U.S. interest in regional political developments. Roosevelt later commented that he was "rather thrilled with the idea of using Iran as an example of what we can do by an unselfish American policy."[3] The idealistic impulse behind those words gave rise to an entire school of "development theory" that wound through U.S. policy in Iran and elsewhere for thirty years, until it disintegrated in the turmoil of the Iranian revolution.

The U.S.-Soviet Rivalry

The first direct confrontation between the United States and the Soviet Union in the postwar era, and one of the opening salvos of the cold war, was the dispute over the withdrawal of Soviet forces from northern Iran in 1946. Although this issue was resolved peacefully by U.S. and British diplomatic pressures in the United Nations, backed by overwhelming U.S. global military power and some adept political maneuvering by the Iranian government, the incident made a vivid impression on the U.S. leadership. From that day to this, Iran has been perceived by several generations of U.S. political leaders as the most likely site outside the European theater where an armed clash with the U.S.S.R. might escalate into a global conflict.

In U.S. strategic planning, the scenario of a Soviet armed attack across Iran toward the Persian Gulf has consistently been used to size American rapid deployment forces and to calculate lift requirements. Reliance on this scenario did not imply that such an attack was regarded as imminent, nor did it lead to the permanent deployment of major forces in the region. Its appeal was that it was not implausible, it involved potential combat against substantial military forces, it raised all the political uncertainties of a third world conflict, and it was located in one of the least accessible places on the globe for U.S. military forces. Hence, it was useful as a stressful scenario to test U.S. military capabilities. Psychologically, however, the familiarity of the Iranian-Persian Gulf scenario meant that U.S. military and government officials perhaps have been more conscious of the Soviet threat in that sector than in other possible trouble spots around the world.

In the 1960s, as the British "long recessional" from its empire became manifest, strategic planners in both the United States and Britain recognized that future capability for power projection in the Indian Ocean would be hampered by the loss of support facilities when the British withdrew. Therefore, they proposed stockpiling some facilities for possible future use. In the Kennedy administration, a study was undertaken to identify "strategic islands" in the Indian Ocean and elsewhere that might be able to serve that purpose. Diego Garcia was one of the islands.

In 1964 the Chagos Archipelago, which included Diego Garcia, was detached from Mauritius and the Seychelles, and in the following year these islands were constituted as the British Indian Ocean Territory (BIOT) by a British Order-in-Council. A U.S.-U.K. executive agreement was signed in 1966 providing for the use of these islands for joint defense purposes.

The strategic rationale for the establishment of BIOT was the perceived need for future support facilities in the context of long-term contingency planning. However, that was insufficient to overcome political opposition in a skeptical U.S. Congress, which was being asked to fund initial construction. Consequently, the executive branch was led to inflate the nature of the political threat by talk of a "power vacuum" in the region and to make the Diego Garcia installation appear to be more significant—and thereby more threatening—than it was in fact.

Construction work on Diego Garcia began in 1971, and by early 1973 the United States had an austere communication station supported by an 8000-foot runway. The perception of expansive U.S. interests had repercussions in the attitudes of the littoral states and, most significantly, in the Soviet Union.

The Naval Rivalry

The British announcement in 1968 of its intent to withdraw its military presence East of Suez by 1971 came at a moment when the U.S.S.R. was beginning to develop a new maritime policy of power projection in areas far from the Soviet land mass. Almost simultaneously with the British announcement, the U.S.S.R. began to deploy naval forces to the region on a regular basis. In 1968, two to four Soviet combat vessels were maintained in the area, together with supporting auxiliaries, for a total of about 1900 ship-days. By 1969, this level had more than doubled to about 4100 ship-days, and it doubled again by 1972 to about 8800 ship-days. The first Soviet submarine appeared in October 1968, and in August of the same year the first reconnaissance flights by Soviet Bear D aircraft occurred. During the same period, General Secretary Leonid Brezhnev launched a political campaign to squeeze Western presence out of Asia. His call for an Asian collective security arrangement attracted no support in the region, but it was generally interpreted by the Western powers as a transparent effort to play on the nationalist sentiment of the regional states and to add a political dimension to the increased Soviet military presence.

In December 1971, regional and Soviet concerns about U.S. intentions were sharply increased when the carrier U.S.S. *Enterprise* and a Seventh Fleet task force were sent into the Bay of Bengal as a gesture of reassurance to Pakistan during their war with India over Bangladesh. This was the first quasi-operational deployment of U.S. forces into the region since the World War II. The Soviets responded with their own deployment of a substantial naval force, including the first introduction of cruise missile submarines to the region.

At the same time, the regional states were undertaking their own effort to prevent the Persian Gulf and Indian Ocean from becoming an arena for superpower military rivalry. A "zone of peace" resolution first passed the U.N. General Assembly in December 1971 calling for "elimination of any manifestation of great power military presence in the Indian Ocean, conceived in the context of great power rivalry." Both the United States and the Soviet Union abstained, as did most of the major maritime nations of the world.

The Two-Pillar Policy

In 1969 on the island of Guam, President Richard Nixon announced what came to be known as the "Nixon Doctrine," which proposed that the United States support and place greater reliance on regional powers to help protect its interests worldwide, at a time when U.S. forces were stretched thin because of Vietnam. Perhaps the clearest translation of this policy into concrete action was in the Persian Gulf, where the United States had significant national interests but was hampered by public opinion and by military overcommitment from developing a regional security policy. As a consequence, enhanced ties of security cooperation were forged with Iran and Saudi Arabia—the so-called "two-pillar" policy.

From the beginning, Iran was acknowledged as the predominant of the two "pillars." President Nixon and Henry Kissinger visited Iran in May 1972 and concluded a series of agreements. In return for Iranian support and protection of U.S. interests in the region, the United States agreed to increase the level of its military advisory presence in Iran and to "accede to any of the Shah's requests for arms purchases from us (other than some sophisticated advanced technology armaments and with the very important exception, of course, of any nuclear weapons capability. . .)."[4] The United States agreed not to "second guess" the Shah, and the U.S. intelligence capabilities in Iran were gradually shifted away from Iranian internal politics to focus almost exclusively on the Soviet Union.

During this same meeting, the United States agreed to cooperate with Iran and Israel in a covert action in support of the Kurdish rebels in northern Iraq, with the objective of bringing pressure on the Baathist government of Saddam Hussein and to divert Iraqi forces away from the Arab-Israeli sector. At the end of his discussions with the Shah, President

Nixon captured the essence of the meeting in just two words. He looked across the table at the Shah and said simply, "Protect me."[5]

The October War

By mid-1973, the United States had every reason to be satisfied with its basic strategy. The political transition to independence by the mini-states of the Persian Gulf following the British withdrawal had been more orderly than almost anyone would have dared hope. The Iranian seizure of the small islands of Abu Musa and the Tunbs at the mouth of the gulf in late 1971 had been balanced by the retraction of Iranian claims to Bahrain, and initial Arab outrage seemed to subside into acceptance of a fait accompli. The Iraqi threat to Kuwait in March 1973 and a nearly simultaneous upsurge of tension between Saudi Arabia and South Yemen were managed without any need for direct U.S. intervention. Both of the two pillars of U.S. policy, Iran and Saudi Arabia, appeared stable and increasingly self-confident. In its role as protecting power, Iran was providing troops to assist the new sultan of Oman to put down the externally-assisted rebellion in Dhofar Province.

Despite the growing importation of oil, the balance of trade between the United States and the Persian Gulf states strongly favored the United States and was expected to stay that way as the oil producers sought Western technology and products with their increasing oil revenues. The U.S. Middle East Force—an auxiliary command ship and two destroyers— seemed securely established after successful negotiation of a lease with the government of Bahrain, replacing the original British host arrangement.

This tranquility was broken by the events resulting from the Arab-Israeli war of 1973. The oil embargo by Arab states against the United States and certain other countries supporting Israel demonstrated that business and politics in the Persian Gulf could not safely be separated form each other. The resulting panic in the world markets, including massive disruption in the U.S. domestic distribution system, created the impression that the United States was much more vulnerable than had been previously supposed. The threat of possible naval actions against shipping destined for Israel drew attention to the vulnerability of oil shipping lanes through the Gulf and the Indian Ocean. The government of Bahrain demanded that U.S forces terminate their use of facilities there.[6]

The United States sent a carrier task force into the Arabian Sea in October as part of a global alert of U.S. forces during the war and maintained a greatly increased naval presence for six months thereafter. Secretary of Defense James Schlesinger subsequently announced that the United States would conduct more frequent and more regular naval deployments to the region, and he requested emergency upgrading of the facility at Diego Garcia. The Soviet Union doubled its warship presence in response to U.S. naval deployments and began development of a major military airfield and missile handling facility at Berbera in Somalia, raising U.S. fears of the imminent introduction of Soviet long-range surveillance and strike aircraft into the region.

Diego Garcia and the Naval Arms Talks

The debate between the administration and Congress over expansion of Diego Garcia was acrimonious and prolonged. In March 1975, President Ford declared, at congressional insistence, that construction of Diego Garcia was "essential to the national interest of the United States." This was the first high-level policy statement to assert that essential U.S. interests were at stake in the Persian Gulf and Indian Ocean regions. Also at congressional insistence, the Ford administration examined the possibility of naval arms limitations talks with the U.S.S.R., concluding that such talks were not warranted. In 1976 work began to equip Diego Garcia with a 12000-foot runway and replenishment facilities to support a carrier task force for sixty days.

The Carter administration continued the policies of its predecessors with respect to force deployments, but unlike President Ford, Carter chose to pursue the possibility of naval arms limitations talks with the U.S.S.R. A framework for such talks had been developed in 1976 in response to congressional prodding, and formal talks began in Moscow in June 1977, followed by sessions in Washington and Bern, Switzerland.

Some progress was made on technical issues, but the key dilemma that emerged from the discussions was the inability of an essentially naval agreement to deal with the more basic issues of regional intervention. This problem was dramatized by the Soviet and Cuban intervention in favor of the Marxist regime in Ethiopia. The talks broke down in early 1978 and remained moribund until the coup de grace was delivered—as it was to other arms-control initiatives—by the Soviet invasion of Afghanistan in December 1979. Moreover, the Soviets lost their key bargaining chip—the sizable air base that they had been building in Somalia—when they sided with Ethiopia against Somalia.

Although the discussions with the Soviets about naval arms limitations produced no agreement, they did provide a useful opportunity for the two sides to discuss in some detail their military activities and objectives in the region. Thus, it became clear to the U.S. negotiators that one of the key Soviet interests in the region was to defend against anticipated deployments of U.S. ballistic missile submarines pointed at the U.S.S.R. across its southern underbelly. The Soviet side, in turn, was able to conclude from these talks that such U.S. ballistic missile deployments were unlikely due to technological developments. In retrospect, it is also apparent that these talks took place at the very time that a debate about the use of naval forces for power projection in distant areas had begun inside the Soviet Union. That debate resulted in the downplaying of such a mission for the Soviet Navy in the Mediterranean Sea and Indian Ocean.[7]

Perhaps for all of these reasons, the Soviet naval presence in the northwest quadrant of the Indian Ocean has remained essentially static from the late 1970s until the present. The

Soviets have not surged forces into the area in response to repeated large U.S. naval deployments to the Arabian Sea, nor even during the invasion of Afghanistan. Contrary to the fears of the mid-1970s, it now appears that the U.S.S.R. does not regard the Persian Gulf region as an arena of naval rivalry with the United States.

Oil

Oil in commercial quantity was first discovered in the Middle East by an Australian, William D'Arcy, in 1908 at Masjid-i-Suleiman at the head of the Persian Gulf in Iran. The first shipload of oil from that field left Abadan and passed through the Strait of Hormuz in 1912. Most of the other major oil fields in Iraq, the eastern province of Saudi Arabia and the Arab principalities of the Gulf were located and developed by European and U.S. companies beginning in the 1930s. However, the importance of Persian Gulf oil in international politics did not emerge until after World War II.

Initially, the vast oil reserves of the Persian Gulf were viewed as important primarily for commercial and financial reasons. The exploration for oil, as well as its extraction, refining, shipment, and marketing were under the control of a small number of giant oil companies—the so-called Seven Sisters—that held concessionary rights; and it was often difficult to distinguish between U.S. interests in Saudi Arabia, for example, and the interests of the Arabian-American Oil Company (ARAMCO).

The enormous profits generated by the oil companies were crucial to the financial health of a number of governments, and some of the most dramatic political developments in the region were directly related to these lucrative operations. Thus, the U.S. covert action in 1953, which overthrew Premier Mohammed Mossadegh and restored the Shah to the throne, was inspired by the British after Mossadegh had nationalized the Anglo-Iranian Oil Company. Although the "countercoup" was justified within the U.S. government as preventing a possible Soviet takeover of Iran, it was not entirely incidental that the action resulted in a new operating consortium in which U.S. companies acquired a 40 percent interest.

OPEC

The Organization of Oil Exporting Countries (OPEC) was originally formed in 1960 to protect producing countries from price fluctuations established by the oil companies. In the early 1970s, when the industrialized world was becoming increasingly dependent on oil as an energy source, OPEC was instrumental in asserting the rights of producer countries to greater participation in the operation of the industry. It was extremely successful. Over the past fifteen years, the gulf states have assumed primary decision-making power over oil, and the role of the companies has increasingly become that of a service industry. The equity interest of the international oil companies in Middle East crude oil production, which nearly equaled that of the host governments at the beginning of the 1970s, had declined to approximately 5 percent by 1980.

This fundamental shift reflected the new realities of the world oil market. From the end of World War II until the mid-1960s, the United States was the largest oil producer in the world and was therefore able to exercise dominant influence on the international oil market. However, U.S. production peaked in the early 1970s and then began to decline, while gulf production soared. By 1979 Saudi production substantially exceeded total U.S. production, and the gulf region was producing nearly three times as much oil as the United States.

As worldwide demand for oil increased, the gulf states, with their massive oil reserves, were in a position to assert greater independent leverage over pricing and production. This new power was vigorously demonstrated in the wake of the October 1973 Arab-Israeli war when the gulf states ordered production cutbacks and imposed a partial oil boycott. This disruption of normal supply patterns and the resulting fears of a global oil shortage permitted OPEC to quadruple the price of oil, from the $2-3 range to nearly $12 a barrel. Further upward pressure was created by the disruptions of the Iranian revolution in 1978-1979, and OPEC followed the spot market to establish a price of about $32 a barrel by mid-1980.

Thus, in one tumultuous decade the entire production and pricing system of international oil was transformed, as was the perception of U.S. and Western interests in the Persian Gulf. The cartel of Western oil companies was broken and replaced by a producers' organization able to exploit upward pressures to the benefit of its members. The role of the United States as key producer and oil exporter was supplanted by the gulf states in general and Saudi Arabia in particular. The strategic dependency of the industrialized states on the oil of the Persian Gulf became manifestly apparent. And the earlier perception of oil as a matter of primarily commercial interest was replaced by a perception of oil as a strategic, political concern.

The U.S. Response

The United States responded to this series of reversals and shattering change by political and strategic improvisation. After the oil shock of 1973-1974, Secretary of Defense James Schlesinger pointedly noted that the United States possessed the necessary military capability to respond if the oil weapon were used to cripple the industrialized world. In November 1974, the carrier *U.S.S. Constellation* broke off from routine exercises in the Arabian Sea and conducted air operations during a 36-hour circumnavigation of the Persian Gulf—the only time a U.S. carrier has ever entered the constricted waters of the gulf. This was followed that December by a *Business Week* interview with Secretary of State Kissinger in which he declared that, in the event of actual "strangulation" of Western economies, the United States could not exclude the use of force. There was talk in the media of a U.S. invasion of the gulf,[8] and the United States raised its level of naval presence in the region, sending alternating deployments of carrier and surface ship task forces to the region every four months. If the object of these maneuvers was to get the undivided attention of the gulf rulers, they certainly succeeded.

Kissinger's brilliant negotiation of Israeli disengagment from the Sinai in 1974-1975 led Anwar Sadat to surprise everyone by abrogating Egypt's treaty with the Soviet Union and moving closer to the United States. This event, plus the reopening of the Suez Canal in 1975, helped create an "anchor to windward" for U.S. Arab policy and greatly increased U.S. capability to insert forces into the region on short notice. The political process of reconciliation with Egypt was intensified and extended by President Carter, whose extraordinary personal diplomacy culminated in the 1978 Camp David Accords and, in 1979, the first peace treaty between an Arab state and Israel.

The sultan of Oman visited Washington in 1975 and agreed to permit U.S. reconnaissance aircraft to operate from Masirah Island off the Omani coast in return for U.S. sale of TOW missiles and other military equipment to Oman. Access to limited military support facilities near the mouth of the Persian Gulf meant that U.S. air surveillance could be sustained on a more regular basis than was possible when operating from Diego Garcia, some 2500 miles away. The United States also increased its sales of arms to Saudi Arabia and other gulf states, over strenuous objections from Israel, to enhance its political ties and to sop up some of the excess oil profits piling up in the oil states.

The Iranian Revolution

At the same time the United States was gaining a new partner in Egypt, it was losing one in Iran. The sudden and total collapse of the Shah's regime in Iran at the end of 1978 effectively demolished a decade of U.S. strategy in the Persian Gulf region. Without Iran, the Nixon Doctrine was invalidated, and the United States was left strategically naked, with no safety net.

This sense of imminent concern was magnified in February 1979 by reports of an incipient invasion of North Yemen by its avowedly Marxist neighbor to the south. This event, coming in the wake of the Marxist coup in Afghanistan in April 1978, the conclusion of the Ethiopian-Soviet treaty in November 1978, the fall of the Shah and the assassination of U.S. Ambassador Adolph Dubs in Kabul in February 1979, created the impression that the United States had lost all capacity to influence regional events. That impression was strengthened when Turkey and Pakistan followed Iran in withdrawing from the Central Treaty Organization in March.

The U.S. government responded to the Yemen crisis with a series of measures intended to reassure American friends in the region and to demonstrate U.S. resolve. A carrier task force was dispatched to the Arabian Sea, establishing a new baseline of constant U.S. military presence for years to come. An emergency package of military aid was rushed to Yemen, and AWACS early warning aircraft were deployed to Saudi Arabia for joint training and to bolster Saudi air defenses.

Over the remainder of 1979, the United States undertook a systematic effort to develop a new "strategic framework" for the Persian Gulf. By the end of 1979, the outlines of a strategy had been sketched in, including initial identification of U.S. forces for a rapid deployment force, operational planning for an increased U.S. military presence, the permanent presence of a carrier in or near the Arabian Sea, and preliminary discussions with Oman, Kenya, and Somalia about possible use of facilities.

Nevertheless, when the U.S. embassy in Teheran was attacked in November, a high-level review of U.S. military capabilities drew the sobering conclusion that U.S. ability to project military power in the region beyond a show of force was extremely limited. In late November, when there were serious fears that the U.S. hostages were in danger of being killed, a second aircraft carrier was sent to the area, and two additional destroyers were assigned to the Middle East Force. Thus, when the next great drama of the region occurred, the United States already had substantial military forces on the scene.

The Invasion of Afghanistan

The Soviet invasion of Afghanistan just before Christmas in 1979 can be explained variously in terms of Soviet interests, perceptions, or strategy. On the U.S. side, however, the result was rather simple. The invasion aroused latent fears of Soviet expansionism that are never very far beneath the surface of U.S. foreign policy.

On this occasion, as in the past, analysts and pundits recalled Molotov's draft amendment to the pact proposed by German Foreign Minister Ribbentropp in 1940 indicating that the center of Soviets aspirations was "the area south of Batum and Baku in the general direction of the Persian Gulf." Similarly, it was remembered that Article VI of the Irano-Soviet Treaty of 1921 sanctioned Soviet intervention in Iran in the event of hostile forces operating there.[9] These two documents are often cited as evidence that the Soviet Union continues to pursue a drive for warm water ports that dates back to the days of the czars.

This image of a Soviet drive to the Persian Gulf and Indian Ocean dominated analyses in both the media and among government officials. The geography of Afghanistan was examined, not so much to discover how difficult it might be for the U.S.S.R. to extend its sway in such a hostile terrain, but rather to demonstrate that air bases constructed in southern and western Afghanistan could extend Soviet air power to the Persian Gulf and Arabian Sea. In short, the Soviet invasion was widely perceived not as a political gambit to preserve a Soviet position in Afghanistan but as an initial step toward more lucrative targets at a time when U.S. power and influence were severely impaired.

The practical effect of the Soviet invasion was to terminate the efforts of the Carter administration to seek mutual accommodation with the Soviet Union, including support for the SALT II treaty. It undercut the consistent efforts of Secretary of State Vance to pursue a low-key negotiating approach with the U.S.S.R. and persuaded President Carter to rely more heavily on the advice of his hawkish advisers, particularly Zbigniew Brzezinski.

The Carter Doctrine and the Birth of the RDJTF

This policy shift was articulated by Carter in his State of the Union address of January 23, 1980, where he stated that "Any attempt by any outside force to gain control of the Persian Gulf region will be regarded as an assault on the vital interests of the United States of America, and such an assault will be repelled by any means necessary, including military force." This declaration, which quickly came to be known as the Carter Doctrine, bore a remarkable resemblance to the classic statement of British policy by Lord Lansdowne in 1903, when he said the United Kingdom would "regard the establishment of a naval base, or of a fortified port, in the Persian Gulf by any other power as a very grave menace to British interests, an act that would be resisted with all the means at our disposal".[10] Carter's statement clearly established the United States as the protector power of the region and effectively completed the transfer of policy responsibility in the Persian Gulf from the British to the Americans.

When Carter made this statement, it reflected U.S. intentions rather than capabilities. Despite the planning that had been conducted over the previous year, the United States was poorly equipped to respond to a major Soviet military challenge in the Persian Gulf region. Over the following year, a number of additional steps were taken, including the formal establishment of a rapid deployment joint task force (RDJTF), deployment of seven prepositioning ships to Diego Garcia, requests to Congress to purchase eight fast roll-on, roll-off ships that could reach the Suez Canal from the U.S. east coast in eleven to twelve days, exercise deployment of some RDJTF forces to Egypt and other countries in the area, and positioning tactical air forces and combat lift for rapid deployment to the area. Access agreements were signed with Oman, Kenya, and Somalia, and talks were initiated with Pakistan on countering the Soviet intervention. An amphibious ready group with 1800 Marines was sent to the Arabian Sea, and AWACS aircraft were deployed to Saudi Arabia to enhance air defenses in the gulf after the outbreak of the Iran-Iraq war.

Despite these efforts, by the time the Reagan administration arrived in Washington in January 1981, it would have been accurate to say that the U.S. security structure in the Persian Gulf region was more symbol than reality—at least as measured in purely military capacity.[11] Nevertheless, it was equally apparent that the developments of 1980 marked a major threshold in the evolution of U.S. strategy and a new conviction that this region represented a major strategic zone of U.S. vital interests, demanding both sustained attention at the highest levels of U.S. policy making and direct U.S. engagement in support of specifically U.S. interests. That was without precedent.

The Central Command

The Reagan administration adopted the Carter Doctrine and over the following seven years succeeded in putting more substantial military power and organization behind its words. The RDJTF was reorganized in 1983 as a unified command known as the Central Command (CENTCOM), based at MacDill Air Force Base in Tampa, Florida, with earmarked forces totaling some 230,000 military personnel from the four services. Its basic mission reflected the two themes that had wound through U.S. regional policy from the very beginning: "to assure continued access to Persian Gulf oil and to prevent the Soviets from acquiring political-military control directly or through proxies."

Its area of responsibility includes East Africa from Egypt to Kenya, the eastern Arab states excluding those on the eastern Mediterranean, as far east as Pakistan. This area, which has always been the "back yard" of U.S. military commands in the Pacific and Europe, with forces "borrowed" from and reporting to their individual headquarters, has now been consolidated under a single operational commander with a single chain of command. Military-to-military relationships have been established with many of the countries in the region, and coordination and some prepositioning of material have proceeded discreetly.

From the beginning of the RDJTF during the Carter administration, it has been recognized that while military force might be able to deter or contain a Soviet thrust southward, it would be less able to deal with the political turmoil and instability of the regional states. That fact remains true. Given a reasonable amount of warning, CENT- COM today could probably prevent the U.S.S.R. from taking the Iranian oil fields in the southern part of the country, though it would probably have to cede the northern part of the country to a determined Soviet advance. The forces available to CENTCOM are also valuable instruments for the United States in pursuing its diplomatic objectives in the area. These forces will not, however, prevent the Soviets from making their own diplomatic intrusions into the gulf, nor will they provide in themselves any guarantee against internal political dissent or instability within the gulf states.

That fact is critical, since the real problem for the United States and other powers with interests in the region has always been more political than military. The Soviet Union had more than four divisions in Afghanistan and another twenty-eight divisions ranged along the Soviet southern frontier that could be used in a military offensive. However, despite the fears generated by the invasion of Afghanistan, there is little credible evidence that the U.S.S.R. is planning any further intervention to the south, at least in the near term. On the contrary, the Soviets have been bloodied in Afghani- stan and seem to be more interested in disentangling them- selves from a costly and untenable situation than in pressing farther toward the Persian Gulf or the Indian Ocean.

Regional Politics and U.S. Interests

Despite the shadow of Soviet military power just north of Iran and Turkey, all of the recent threats to oil supplies and to regional stability have come not from the U.S.S.R. but from indigenous political developments within the region. The most dangerous of these threats has been the Iran-Iraq war, which Iraq launched with a massive invasion in September 1980. Iran drove Iraqi troops back to the frontier by 1982 and then attempted to push across the border. Although Iran succeeded in taking the Fao Peninsula in 1986, the war has been essentially a stalemate for nearly six years.

At the beginning of the war, the United States asserted its neutrality, though it tended to tilt toward Iraq. In 1985-1986, in an abortive effort to free U.S. hostages in Lebanon, the United States and Israel undertook a series of secret contacts and substantial arms transfers to Iran that effectively shifted U.S. policy—at least at the covert level—toward Iran. When the revelation of these arrangements created consternation and threatened U.S. relations with the friendly oil-producing states of the gulf, the United States reversed field sharply and adopted a pro-Iraqi position.

The Tanker War

During much of the war, the United States and many other powers took a hands-off posture on the grounds that they could have little effect on the outcome of the conflict and since it was having relatively little impact on oil supplies. That began to change in 1985-1986 when Iran began to retaliate for Iraqi air attacks against its shipping in the gulf by using mines and small armed boats against neutral shipping en route to Kuwait and Saudi Arabia.

In late 1986, Kuwait asked both the United States and the Soviet Union to place Kuwaiti tankers under their flag and provide protection. The Soviet Union agreed to reflag three Kuwaiti tankers, and the United States quickly followed suit by reflagging eleven. The United States moved a substantial number of naval ships into or near the gulf and began escorting tanker convoys to and from Kuwait.[12] Iran's indiscriminate use of mines led other NATO navies (France, Great Britain, Italy, Belgium, and the Netherlands) to send minesweepers and other escort ships to the gulf to protect international shipping. By the end of 1987 the convoy operation appeared to have settled into a nervous routine, and the United States was considering some reductions in its naval forces.

International Diplomacy and the Iran-Iraq War

"If the Iran-Iraq war does not come to an end officially in 1988, it will at least be practically over." This judgment, so contrary to the prevailing image of the war as a conflict without end, was expressed not by an armchair observer from afar but by Crown Prince Abdallah of Saudi Arabia, who had just completed a round of consultations about the war in the major Arab capitals followed by a summit meeting of Arab Gulf states.[13] His view is still very much a minority perspective, but there is growing evidence that this seemingly interminable war may be winding down at last.

One year earlier, Iran was engaged in a massive offensive, "Karbala V," designed to break through the formidable Iraqi defenses around the southern city of Basra. That offensive, which had been in preparation for an entire year, was arguably the best-prepared, best-armed and most skillfully conducted operation in the long history of this brutal conflict. In the preceding year, Iran had succeeded in acquiring new arms and spare parts from the United States and Israel as a result of the Iran-Contra affair, in addition to military supplies from China and a number of other sources. The Iranian military, after more than eight years of battle, had achieved a new level of competence and professionalism, and Iran's political leadership was prepared to commit the full resources of the country in the pursuit of a decisive victory that would topple the regime of President Saddam Hussein in Iraq.

It failed. Iraqi defensive lines held firm against the onslaught. Iraq now celebrates its successful resistance as the "Great Day" of battle, while Iran was forced to reconsider its entire military strategy. The Iranian leadership had to ask themselves whether one more offensive was likely to succeed where the supreme effort had failed.

In the end, Iran chose quietly to adopt a new approach. In June 1987 Mohsen Rezaie, the military commander of Iran's Revolutionary Guards, announced in a little-noticed interview that Iran's military plans for the coming year would involve not a massive single offensive as in the past but a "series of limited operations and a series of bigger ones. . . . We have plans to organize, train and arm popular forces inside Iraq. . . . This is the new front."[14]

This new strategy, which was subsequently espoused by all key Iranian leaders, had two practical consequences. First, Iran began to arm and train Kurdish forces for sustained guerrilla operations with Revolutionary Guards in northern Iraq. Second, Iran failed to put in place the infrastructure and meticulous planning required for a major new offensive against Basra in the winter of 1987-1988.

The new strategy had implications for Iran's diplomatic strategy as well. On July 20, 1987, the United Nations Security Council unanimously voted a binding resolution calling for an end to the war. It was an open secret in the U.N. that this resolution was intended to lend support to Iraq and to punish Iran. The first paragraph of Resolution 598 demands an immediate cease-fire and withdrawal of forces before the negotiation of outstanding issues between the warring parties. Since Iran was the only party holding substantial territory outside its own borders—the Fao Peninsula that had been taken in February 1986—this meant that Iran was expected to relinquish its major bargaining lever before negotiations started. It was therefore anticipated that Iran would reject the resolution, thereby triggering a second resolution to impose an embargo.

To the surprise of many, Iran did not reject the resolution. Instead, Iran fixed on paragraph six of the resolution that provided for an impartial commission to determine who started the war. If such a commission were established, Iranian officials told U.N. Secretary General Javier Pérez de Cuellar, they would be prepared to observe an informal cease-fire while the panel conducted its investigation.[15] Iran and most other observers believe that Iraq initiated the war in September 1980 with its massive invasion into the Iranian province of Khuzestan, though Iraq insists the attack was provoked.

Iran has chafed at the initial failure of the Security Council to identify Iraq as the aggressor in 1980 and its failure to call for the withdrawal of Iraqi forces. The commission would, in Iranian eyes, rectify this situation and lay the basis for Iranian claims for war reparations. Iraq, needless to say, has stiffly resisted Iran's diplomatic efforts, insisting that Resolution 598 must be implemented strictly in the order of the paragraphs as originally written.

This negotiating process came to an abrupt halt in late 1987, with a measured exchange of military blows between the United States and Iran in the Gulf. This escalatory cycle began on September 21 with the U.S. attack on an Iranian mine-laying ship and ended essentially in a draw with the Iranian missile attack on an oil-loading platform in Kuwaiti waters on October 22. During that period, Iran hardened its negotiating position and hastily announced a mobilization of popular forces for a possible new winter offensive.

By the end of December, tempers had cooled. Iran, perhaps realizing that an unprepared offensive would be futile, let it be known that it was prepared to call off its attack, and talks began with the Arab states of the gulf. It now appears that this will be the first winter in the entire history of the war in which there will be no large military offensive on either side.

In fact, the ground war over the past year has been confined to occasional skirmishes of little strategic significance. Iran is devoting most of its attention to small scale guerrilla operations in Kurdish areas of northern Iraq, while Iraq concentrates on missile attacks against Iranian oil shipping. It would be only a slight exaggeration to say that a fitful and tacit cease-fire has emerged along the main war fronts while the principal focus of the fighting has moved to the shipping lanes of the Persian Gulf.

This brief analysis suggests that Crown Prince Abdallah's comments about a practical end to the war in 1988 may be more than wishful thinking. The Iran-Iraq war, at least for the time being, appears to have settled into a jockeying match by the two warring parties about the order in which the terms of Resolution 598 are to be implemented. That would not seem to be an insuperable problem for creative international diplomacy. The Secretary General has already tabled—and the Security Council has endorsed—a nine-point plan that could provide the basis for a compromise. At a minimum, the prospects for fruitful negotiations would appear sufficiently promising to justify a new visit to the region, either by Secretary General Pérez de Cuellar or by a special representative that he could appoint, just as he has done with the Afghanistan talks.

Some Observations

One of the most startling lessons to be drawn from the turbulence of the past two decades in the gulf has been the relative stability of the oil trade even in the face of massive political and military disturbances. It is worth recalling that, in a period of less than ten years, the following events have occurred:

- The Shah's regime collapsed and was replaced by a radical, anti-Western, theocratic regime, thereby removing the principal pillar of U.S. Persian Gulf policy,
- The Arab states of the Persian Gulf were threatened by a wave of Islamic fundamentalism, including an attempted coup in Bahrain and two major attacks at the holy places in Mecca,
- U.S. diplomatic personnel were taken hostage in Teheran and held for 444 days, including an abortive attempt by the United States to rescue them by military force,
- The Soviet Union sent more than 100,000 troops into Afghanistan, its first military intervention in the region since World War II,

- A vicious war broke out between Iran and Iraq, two of the most important oil producers in the gulf,
- The war eventually spread from the land to attacks on tanker traffic in the gulf, including the widespread use of mines,
- Missile attacks and terrorist bombings were conducted against Kuwait,
- NATO navies sent more than 80 ships to the gulf.

If anyone had predicted this series of events in 1978, it would have been reasonable to expect a dramatic reduction of the flow of oil from the gulf, massive disruptions of supply, and huge increases in the price of oil. In reality, the flow of oil from the gulf has continued at a remarkably steady rate, international oil markets have managed to deal with the crises with little or no serious interruption of supplies, by the end of 1987 there was a glut of oil in world markets, and oil prices, after a sharp increase returned to a point not far above where they began ten years ago. It must be added that this benign interpretation of events is more apparent in retrospect than it was at the time. The psychological reactions to these events produced sharp swings in prices and raised fears of an oil shortage that translated into long gas lines in the United States. Nevertheless, with benefit of hindsight, we have learned that the structure of oil production and marketing in the gulf is considerably more robust than previously supposed.

The Soviet Union, which might have been expected to benefit from these troubling events, has made only marginal progress in its political relationships with the gulf states. On the military side, its intervention in Afghanistan is increasingly regarded—by the Soviets and others—as a failure, and the trend today appears to be toward disengagement rather than further adventures.

None of this is cause for complacency. Quite the contrary. The world has discovered just how unpredictable and dangerous events in that part of the world can be. But as we acknowledge the dangers, we would also be wise to bear in mind the fact that the political and economic structures of the gulf have proven themselves to be unexpectedly sturdy.

One unexpected product of the Iran-Iraq war was the creation of the Gulf Cooperation Council in 1981, establishing a forum for the six Arab gulf states to coordinate their political, economic, and security policies. In its first seven years of existence, the GCC has emerged as an important mechanism to promote stability and cooperation among the gulf states.

On the oil front, the war has encouraged accelerated construction of a series of oil pipelines from the gulf to the Mediterranean and Red Sea. By the end of 1987, these lines were capable of transporting half of the approximately 9 million barrels per day of oil produced in the Persian Gulf. By the end of 1989, pipeline capacity is expected to increase to nearly two-thirds of current gulf production.[16] This development has substantially reduced the dangers of a closure of the Strait of Hormuz by providing alternative outlets.

In terms of great power interests, the events of the past decade have altered perceptions, expectations, and policy implementation. To the extent that great power presence provided some timely reassurance to beleaguered, friendly governments in the gulf, it probably contributed to a positive outcome. But the record of the great powers is so replete with examples of clumsiness, miscalculation, shortsightedness, and even perverse defiance of their own self-interest that it would be a mistake to attribute to them greater importance than they deserve.

In the final analysis, Western interests have been and will be protected not by fleets and troops but by the congruence of those interests with the objectives of the regional states themselves. The gulf states wish to sell their oil and avoid the domination of their powerful neighbor to the north. That reality provides the basis of a sensible and successful policy and endows it with a substantial margin for error.

We have needed that margin in the past. No doubt we will again.

Notes

1. Some of the following background material was adapted from Gary Sick, "The Evolution of U.S. Strategy Toward the Indian Ocean and Persian Gulf Regions," in Alvin Rubinstein, ed., *The Great Game: Rivalry in the Persian Gulf and South Asia*, (New York: Praeger, 1983) pp. 49-80.

2. One aspect of U.S. policy, which differs from the British experience, is the constant competition in U.S. policy between oil interests in the Persian Gulf and interest in the security of Israel. The tension between these two competing interests has been a constant and important element in U.S. decision-making on Middle East issues that must be acknowledged but cannot be examined in any detail in this paper.

3. FDR memorandum to the secretary of state, January 12, 1944. Cited in Bruce R. Kuniholm, *The Origins of the Cold War in the Near East*, (Princeton University Press, 1980) p. 169.

4. Kissinger memorandum to Nixon in 1973, cited in Gary Sick, *All Fall Down: America's Tragic Encounter With Iran*, (New York: Random House, 1985) p.15.

5. *Ibid.*, p.14.

6. A new lease, at substantially increased cost, was negotiated with the Government of Bahrain in 1975.

7. For a useful discussion of this debate and its outcome, see Francis Fukuyama, "Soviet Civil-Military Relations and the Power Projection Mission," Rand Report R-3504-AF, April 1987.

8. See, for example, Robert Tucker, "Oil: The Issue of American Intervention," *Commentary*, (March 1975) and subsequent rejoinders.

9. This article, which was originally aimed at Russian counterrevolutionary forces, was invoked by the U.S.S.R. in its occupation of Iran at the beginning of World War II. Although Iran has repeatedly declared this article void, the Soviet Union has never renounced it.

10. Cited in J.C. Hurewitz, *The Persian Gulf After Iran's Revolution*, Foreign Policy Association Headline Series 244, April 1979, p.22.

11. Former Secretary of Defense James Schlesinger drew attention to this fact in an article questioning whether the RDJTF was rapid, deployable, or even a force. See "Rapid (?) Deployment (?) Force (?)," *Washington Post*, September 24, 1980.

12. The substantial deployment of U.S. forces to the gulf was hastened as was Congressional approval by the Iraqi missile attack on the USS *Stark* on May 17, 1987. Although the buildup was intended to counter Iran, the Iraqi attack galvanized public attention and underlined the threat to shipping in the gulf.

13. Interview with the *Arab Times*, cited in Foreign Broadcast Information Service, *Daily Report: Near East and South Asia*, January 11, 1988.

14. Interview with *Keyhan* newspaper, June 29, 1987, cited in Foreign Broadcast Information Service, *Daily Report: Near East and South Asia*, July 7, 1987.
15. The confidential "Statement by the Secretary-General on his Mission to Iran and Iraq at Security Council Consultations on 16 September 1987" was published in full by the Kuwait News Agency on September 19, 1987. See Foreign Broadcast Information Service, *Daily Report: Near East and South Asia*, September 19, 1987.
16. See, for example, *The Economist*, January 30, 1988, p. 34. Significantly, Iran remains totally dependent on sea transport through the Strait of Hormuz, though it is actively considering construction of a pipeline from its southern oil field to the port of Iskenderun in Turkey.

A Japanese Perspective

Hisahiko Okazaki

This paper was prepared for presentation at a March 1988 Study Group. It has not been revised to reflect the cease-fire that has taken effect in the Persian Gulf war.

The Middle East is a vital region for the Western world. Its importance derives mainly from three factors: oil, geostrategic position, and unique religious, linguistic, and ethnic characteristics.

Oil

That oil is important is not a novel observation. The events of the past decades simply demonstrate that fact. A review of developments since the beginning of the 1980s, however, may shed new light on the ability of the Gulf OPEC nations to influence future supply and demand in the world oil market. In short, the lesson we learnt in the 80s is that we have to acknowledge that the gulf countries will dominate the oil policy of OPEC, as well as the policy of oil producers of the world, for the foreseeable future.

The strength of the gulf countries, especially Saudi Arabia and Kuwait, stems from the following: (1) vast reserves, (2) great and flexible production capabilities, (3) extremely cheap production costs, and (4) comfortable financial circumstances, with a vast revenue potential and a small population to support.

During the period 1982-1985 Saudi Arabia tried to maintain the high price of oil almost single-handedly, accepting the role of "swing-producer" at the sacrifice of its own revenue. Saudi Arabia could afford to play such a role because of its vast foreign exchange reserves and its ability to reduce the

43

size of its budget by scaling down its investment in infrastructure.

Saudi Arabia persisted in this honorable effort for several years but finally realized that it would be futile to continue. Even if total OPEC production was kept low through Saudi Arabia's sacrifice, non-OPEC countries could—and did—increase their production, taking full advantage of the favorable conditions under which the Saudis' swing-producer policy artificially sustained the high price of oil. It finally became apparent that Saudi Arabia alone could not sustain the price. At that time world oil experts asserted that OPEC had collapsed and would have no significant influence for the future.

The events in 1986, however, showed the formidable pressure that Saudi Arabia could exert on the world oil market. During 1981-1985 Saudi Arabia relied only on the fourth of the just cited elements of strength: its foreign assets. However, in 1985-1986 Saudi Arabia employed all four. Saudi Arabia waged a determined fight to regain its share of the world market. Its weapons are most impressive since Saudi Arabia (1) has no fear of the drain of its oil resources, (2) can double or redouble its production on short notice, (3) can undercut competition by producing oil at a cost of less than two dollars a barrel and (4) can survive the severest financial crisis by simply reducing its foreign exchange reserves and cutting the budget.

Nobody could compete effectively against Saudi Arabia, and the fight was over in a comparatively short period. Prices fell below $10 per barrel, and no oil producer could continue the price competition any longer. OPEC members accepted a reasonable fixed price and the responsibility to observe a production ceiling. Nor had non-OPEC producers any more courage to undercut the OPEC price at the risk of another price collapse. Thus, contrary to the pessimistic forecast of many oil experts, order was restored in the oil market.

The lesson of 1986 is expected to stay with oil-producing countries for some time to come. Whenever they are tempted to gain additional market share by undercutting the price, they will be compelled to calculate whether they are doing something to displease Saudi Arabia. Therefore, since then, the price drift has been limited to a very narrow range.

We can assume that Saudi oil policy, after trial and error in the first half of the 1980s, has finally settled on a relatively cheap and stable oil price. In fact this has always been the basic Saudi policy, except for the period of quixotic effort of 1981-1985. The Saudi way of thinking is that oil price should be stable and cheap enough to discourage the fast development of alternative energy sources that may reduce the demand for oil. Furthermore, the Saudi national budget seems to be satisfactorily financed by the current oil revenue at a low and stable price.

As long as Saudi Arabia maintains the policy of holding to a low, stable price, it is hard for anyone to challenge it, although outsiders have effective means to counter a high-price policy. And anyone planning to explore alternative energy sources or even a new oil field has to take into account the fact that the commercial success of the project could always be undermined by the possible price collapse, which Saudi Arabia is capable of engineering at any given time.

Thus, energy supply capacity, particularly that of oil, will not grow significantly in the coming years, in spite of the inevitable steady growth of demand. Assuming that the annual growth of the oil demand is a minimum 1 percent of total world demand of 60 million B.D., the demand will grow by 2 million B.D. in three years. So if Saudi Arabia maintains its low-price policy, the demand-supply relationship is expected to become tighter every year.

We therefore have to accept the prospect that the gulf countries and the other OPEC producers will exercise a significant influence on the world oil market in the future and that their efforts will be successful in maintaining the demand of oil as the main energy source. The crucial implication of the above analysis is that it would be wrong to base Western policy on the belief that the importance of the Middle East as the main supplier of oil and main determinant of world oil price will decrease in the near future.

In the context of East-West rivalry, the West can never afford to lose the gulf area. The United States could afford to lose Cuba, Vietnam, Laos, and so on, but not the gulf. The Carter Doctrine is the expression of this reality. The Soviet Union, knowing that any armed intervention in the gulf would be a *casus belli*, is expected to be cautious in the region. This does not, however, prevent the Soviet Union from taking advantage of any regional turmoil, or from intervening directly after a global East-West confrontation has begun.

As for Japan's policy vis-à-vis the Middle East, it has developed significant safeguards to protect itself against an oil crisis arising from the situation in the region.

Following the first oil shock, Japan started to build its oil stockpile. By 1987 the Japanese oil stockpile had reached the equivalent of 140 days—a quite substantial level. Since Japanese dependency on the oil coming through the Strait of Hormuz is about 50 percent, in the event of its closure, Japan would have oil supplies sufficient to last 280 days. Moreover, under the present circumstances of excess oil producing capacity in the world, it is expected that other countries would increase their oil production in the event of a Middle Eastern crisis. With the availability of such additional sup- plies, Japanese oil experts believe that Japan could survive for 460 days following the closure of the Strait of Hormuz. Some people estimate an even longer period because they are confident that Japan could successfully compete for the remaining available crude oil in the world market as long as other sources were not physically closed by simultaneous crises. Thus, for the short term, Japan's vulnerability has been greatly reduced.

Even in the long term, Japan's structural dependency on oil has been drastically reduced since the first oil shock. Japan has endeavored to shift to an energy-saving economic struc- ture, reducing the per capita requirement for energy by about 30 percent. Before 1973 it was an axiom that energy consump- tion grows parallel with the growth of GNP, but between 1973 and 1985, GNP increased around 60 percent, while energy consumption by Japanese industries decreased by 10 percent. Besides, the share of oil as an energy source came down from 77.6 percent in 1973 to 55.2 percent in 1985. There has also been geographic diversification. In 1973, 76 percent of the crude oil for Japan came from the Middle East, but in 1986 the figure was about 69 percent. Since this trend is expected to continue, Japan will be even less vulnerable to a crisis in the Middle East.

Even with these achievements, however, the fact remains that Japan relies on oil for 55 percent of its energy supply, and about 55 percent (depending on the use of the East-West Pipe Line) of its crude oil comes through the Strait of Hormuz. Therefore, although Japan is no longer vulnerable to the short-term disruption of oil supply from the gulf either by military or political contingencies, it has to still face the fact of its long-term dependency on gulf oil. Japan must therefore prevent the gulf region from falling under Communist influence or a regime permanently hostile to it.

Japan's basic policy is to maintain long-term friendly relations with the gulf nations. This policy should be based on the economies of both Japan and the Middle East states, as well as on long-term political considerations. The Middle East will be the main supplier of oil to Japan for some time to come, while, in turn, Japan will remain the largest market for Middle Eastern countries and the biggest source of their national revenue. A simple calculation indicates that the dependency of national revenue on oil sale to Japan in 1985 was 22 percent for Saudi Arabia, 41 percent for UAE, and 52 percent for both Qatar and Oman. Recognition of interdependence should be the basis of long-term relations between Japan and the gulf countries; they should be aware that both sides will be hurt seriously if existing friendly relations are disrupted by political differences.

In its political relations with the Middle East states, Japan has few problems. Japan has no colonial past in this region. Differences may develop from time to time when Japan has to take sides on various U.N. or other international issues, but rarely do these problems in international forums seriously affect bilateral relations with each of the Middle Eastern countries.

Freed from fear of short-term disruption of friendly relations, both sides can concentrate on the enhancement of mutual understanding. This understanding can be promoted by exchanges of people, leading to efforts to determine the best form of economic cooperation and the identification of long-term common political interests.

As a result of recent developments in the gulf, a new problem has arisen: that of Japan's security policy in connection with its Middle Eastern policy. The problem is whether Japan should take part in the concerted Western operation to escort oil tankers in the gulf. The issue has been posed as one of solidarity with the Western alliance rather than of direct defense of Japan's oil lines. There is no question of Japan's capabilities. Japan has perhaps the largest and the most experienced minesweeping fleet in the world because of its geography and because of its Second World War experience. Nor is there any question of a consensus within the government that U.S.-Japan cooperation is a vital part of Japan's foreign policy. The problems for Japan are: (1) it has a self-imposed restraint on the dispatch of its forces abroad for belligerent purposes, and (2) it has friendly relations with both Iran and Iraq and sees its role as one of inducing Iran to a more moderate policy without the use of force.

Former Prime Minister Nakasone partially overcame these difficulties but at the last moment was deterred from dispatching the fleet by concern over residual pacifist sentiment in part of the governing Liberal Democratic Party. Instead, he decided to help establish a high accuracy navigation system for the gulf. In this way Japan has so far succeeded in making at least a token contribution to the security of navigation in the gulf without a confrontation with Iran.

Geostrategic Position

The Middle East is geostrategically an area of considerable interest for the Soviet Union and is therefore potentially the most volatile and important theater for East-West rivalry.

One Soviet interest in the region derives from the fact that the Middle East offers a potential access to the Indian Ocean. Japan, perhaps together with nineteenth-century Turkey, has had the most historical experience in dealing with Russian efforts to gain access to an open sea. The Russian approach has been both consistent and persistent, based on a very long-term policy. Since the Russians have always had a long-term policy to reach an open sea, the Soviets will never miss an opportunity to exploit an international turmoil to this end.

Nevertheless, compared with access to the Pacific Ocean, the North Atlantic, and the Mediterranean, the priority of access to the south has not been very high for the Soviet Union. The only occasion when the Middle East had the highest priority for the Soviets was during the Second World War. With the Eastern and Western approaches of the Soviet Union blocked by Germany and Japan, the Soviet Union had to rely on a maritime supply line through Iran.

The reason for this low priority is mainly the poor accessibility of the area. In order to reach the Indian Ocean, the Soviets would have to violate Iranian sovereignty by crossing part of Iran, whereas the Soviet interest is mainly in the area surrounding the various straits in the Far East or in Europe. The Soviets moved closest to points near the Indian Ocean when they helped establish the Azerbaijan and Kurdish republics immediately after the Second World War, and later, when they were confident that they could control the southern part of Afghanistan at the beginning of its invasion of that country. However, the Soviet Union would still have to cross two additional barriers before reaching the sea: in the former case, Khuzestan, which is a vital oil producing area for Iran; and in the latter, Baluchestan, which Pakistan and Iran would certainly defend.

Although the southern flank is the hardest route by which the Soviet Union could reach the sea, it is also the most volatile region. On the western and eastern flanks of the Soviet Union, the actual East-West dividing lines have long been fixed because of the Second World War and also the establishment of the People's Republic of China. In the

Middle East, however, the East-West border line is still unclear after the lapsing of CENTO. Further, the internal situations of the regional states are still far from being stable. Therefore, the Middle East is an area of high probability, although low priority, for Soviet intervention. Thus, the region requires constant attention and careful handling in light of consistent Soviet interests.

The Middle East is one of the weakest points for the defense of the Soviet Union. Soviet colonial policy has been harsh and thorough. The Soviets solved the security question of the maritime province in the Far East by forcibly migrating their Korean minority peoples to Central Asia, thus eradicating the problem of the same race living on both sides of the Soviet-Korean border. In Central Asia, Turkmans, Uzbeks, Tadziks, and Kirghiz are living on both sides of Soviet-Afghan border, and, in Azerbaijan, Turks on the Soviet-Iranian border. It is impossible to force the migration of entire Muslim populations to other parts of the Soviet Union. Thus the Soviet Union is under the constant threat of Islamic influence infiltrating from the non-Communist Middle East to Soviet Central Asia. This threat must appear particularly serious in this age of resurgent Islamic fundamentalism. The fact that the Soviet Union is facing a threat leads to the real possibility of their becoming oversensitive and overreactive to developments in neighboring areas.

These facts indicate that the Middle East is potentially the most crucial theater for East-West rivalry. For reasons that have been partly discussed above and are to be treated more in detail in the next section, the Western strategic approach to this East-West rivalry in the Middle East must be, however, quite different from the NATO and Northeast Asian theaters. In short, the approach should be primarily political, with a view to achieving and maintaining an equilibrium in the region. The possible range of contingencies are far more varied than in the NATO theater. All the possible developments spring from prevailing political situations, and measures to restore equilibrium are, therefore, required to be primarily political and nonmilitary, at least until the final phase of confrontation.

As long as an equilibrium is maintained, the Soviet Union will have very little chance to expand its influence in the region. Arab nations, as we will see in the next part of this paper, clearly distinguish between alien forces and their own, and are never willing to accept external influence unless it is absolutely necessary for their security.

For the same reason, an equilibrium should be achieved primarily by a balance of initiatives and forces intrinsic to the region. The nations of the region reject external forces as permanent elements of regional equilibrium. External forces may be required from time to time, or even for an extended period as in the case of Syria and South Yemen, but they are nevertheless perceived as forces which come and go.

Religious, Linguistic, and Ethnic Characteristics

The Arab Islamic peoples constitute a unique independent world. In the past, various doubts have been cast on the proposition that the Arab world is one. Some people argue that without the Palestinian problem the Arab world would be hopelessly divided and, therefore, they urge a solution to the problem, which is not a bad proposal in itself.

It is true that the interests of Arab nations are divided, but most of the causes of the division come from the history of colonization and the processes by which nations acquired independence.

The Middle East Islamic world has established great unified empires quite a few times in history and still has strong potential centripetal elements, the most important of which are religion, language, and way of thinking. And all these three are actually one.

First of all, Arabs have a religion that is essentially a way of life as well as the most strictly observed in the modern world. The basic text is the Koran that is recited intensively with powerful effects. Egypt, for example, had its original language completely replaced by Arabic in spite of a civilization dating back several thousand years. This is a clear contrast to China, whose civilization and language survived Mongolian and Manchurian conquest and even assimilated the conquerors. It is assumed that this strange phenomenon was a result of the practice of reciting the Koran. The Koran is written in the most rhythmical, powerful, and artistic language. Therefore, through the use of language, it has influenced the way of thinking of all Arabic-speaking people. It is remarkable that so many people in such a wide area have the same religion, speak the same language, and think the same way.

Even the gulf monarchs feel more affinity toward Palestinian revolutionaries than toward Western conservatives. This affinity is among people educated by the Koran and who practice prayer, fasting and pilgrimage to Mecca.

Unified, Arabs would represent a redoubtable power. With a population of about 150 million, Arab countries occupy an area bigger than China. As in the case of China, it is essential for the rest of the world to determine the place that the Arab world should occupy in the international community and in the world balance of power. It is therefore essential for both East-West powers to establish a relationship of mutual accommodation.

The Western knowledge of the Arab world, compared to its knowledge of China, is appallingly limited. This is still more surprising when we consider that Western association with the Middle East has a much longer history than with the Far East. Actually one of the most frequent complaints heard in the Middle East is that the Western world does not try to understand Arab culture and its way of thinking; rather, the West criticizes the Arab way of life. By contrast, the West recognizes that it has an obligation to understand and come to terms with China and Chinese civilization.

The Arab Islamic world lacked unity both during and after the colonial period. Also, in the recent centuries, Arabs did not move toward the industrialization that has been the source of power in the modern world. But the aspiration for Arab unity remains. In the United Nations the Arab nations succeeded in forming an influential bloc against Israel in alliance with anti-apartheid Africans. In 1973, the Arab oil-producing countries made a tremendous impact on the Western nations by the threat of an oil embargo. These two examples are evidence that the Arab world has the will and the capacity to execute unified action with whatever weapons are available.

In conclusion, one has to base an Arab policy on the recognition that the Arabs have their own world, with its unique civilization and extremely homogeneous way of thinking. One cannot apply conventional criteria of East-West relations or North-South relations to the Arab world. Rather, the West should accept it as it is and try to achieve mutual accommodations.

The importance of mutual accommodations is quite often neglected because of the existing divisions among the Arab states, which make them highly vulnerable to manipulation by outside powers. Also, there was a postwar period—the period of Nasserism—when political ideology played a greater role in Arab thinking than religious or traditional concerns. But even in Egypt, the most dynamic revolutionary element these days is that of Islamic fundamentalism. In the past, for example, Winston Churchill, who was confident in his dealings with Saudi Arabia, encountered a sharp "no" from King Abdul Aziz on the recognition of Israel. And Soviet influence did not last in Egypt and is declining in Iraq.

The Arab world is essentially immune to Communism. According to Islamic doctrine, atheists, such as Communists, should be destroyed, while Christians and Jews should be accommodated as the "People of the Book." In that sense, the Arab world has the potential to become a natural friend of the Western Christian world and to become an important element in the balance of power in the world, but only if the nations comprising the Arab world are understood and treated with respect.

The Soviet Union may also be well aware of this fact, having learned valuable lessons from its experiences in Egypt and Afghanistan. The Soviet Union has also had difficulties in imposing its will on Syria, sometimes even on South Yemen.

Since its expulsion from Egypt, the Soviet Union seems to be taking a "wait-and-see" position in the Middle East, apart from the forced continuous engagement in Afghanistan. As long as the general situation is under control, the West may expect the Soviet Union to maintain its current careful, or rather inactive, approach to the region.

Only in the following cases must we be watchful for Soviet moves. The first is the case in which a Middle Eastern nation feels its vital security is threatened and finds no help coming from any source other than the Soviet Union.

The second case is where a central government is so weakened that minorities claim their independence and seek arms for that purpose, as in the case of Kurdistan in 1946. Usually Western nations are reluctant to give this kind of assistance, which is illegal under international law. Communist countries tend to be the main supplier. They then expand their influence by sending a military assistance mission and by asking the minority movement to form a kind of government that the Soviet Union is more than willing to assist. It is noteworthy that Iran could be a potential candidate for Soviet involvement in both cases, depending on the future development of the gulf war. With Iraq, it is more likely that the government would seek the help of other Arab states and the West in the first case, and that Iraqi minorities seek support from Iran rather than the Soviets in the second case.

The Gulf Question

In the discussion of the current gulf war and the existing Western options, the analogy of China may again be valid. During the past seven years of the conflict, the international community had taken a somewhat detached attitude. Many countries thought that a state of conflict with no winners was not at all uncomfortable. Quite recently, however, the Arab world, and perhaps the entire world, seems to be concerned over the prospect of a possible Iranian victory over Iraq.

The gulf countries fear that fundamentalist, antimonarchic fervor will spread among their Shiite populations, thus undermining security, if not leading to direct invasion by victorious Iranian forces. This apprehension over a possible Iranian victory is not limited only to the gulf area. The fundamentalists are becoming restive and their influence is growing in every Arab country. An Iranian victory is feared, as it might encourage increased fundamentalist activities among Arab Muslims, whether they are Sunni or Shiite.

This situation is reminiscent of Southeast Asia in 1965. China was considered to be a fanatical and convinced expansionist force, with its revolutionary fervor and its world strategy of "People's Liberation." Although there is no way to prove that the so-called domino theory was correct, if the 1965 Indonesian coup d'état attempt had been successful, the whole of Southeast Asia would have certainly been placed under the influence of the Peking/Phnom Penh/Jakarta axis. The Malaysian and Singaporean regimes would have come under severe pressure from the Communist-orientated elements of their Chinese populations, and Thailand would have been neutralized. It is hard to know how plausible the fundamentalist domino theory is in the Middle East today, but the atmosphere is almost the same.

The American answer in 1965 was intervention in Vietnam. Again, assessment of the effect of the U.S. intervention in Vietnam is still divided. Americans certainly failed to achieve their primary purpose of preventing the Indo-Chinese countries from falling under Communist control. American intervention also worsened the prolonged Sino-American confrontation, in spite of the fact that China was already under severe pressure from the Soviet Union as the Sino-Soviet rift deepened.

On the other hand, American intervention in Vietnam helped achieve the prosperity and stability of the rest of Asia. American determination to intervene militarily in Vietnam countered defeatism and Marxist fatalism in Southeast Asian countries, above all in Thailand, Malaysia, and Singapore. For ten years, there was remarkable progress toward economic and political stability in these Southeast Asian countries. As Lee Kuan Yu said, "American intervention bought precious time for improving political and economic resilience among these countries." The Association of Southeast Asian Nations (ASEAN) was formed in 1967. Today the area is one of the most prosperous and fastest growing in the world.

If we can draw any lesson from the consequences of the American intervention in Vietnam, it would be to try and maximize the advantage to be gained by intervention and to minimize the problems it creates. In a word, American intervention should contribute to the improvement of political and economic stability in the gulf region, help promote regional cooperation, and avoid confrontation with Iran.

The GCC is one of the finest political achievements of the gulf countries since their independence. The small gulf nations had been wary of Saudi domination, because of the historical fact that they owe their independence to the British intervention that prevented Saudi influence from reaching them in the 1910s and 1920s. However, GCC (Gulf Cooperation Council) countries have gradually accepted the notion of regional cooperation, partly because they have come to trust peaceful, careful, and low-profile Saudi diplomacy, and partly because of the Iranian threat. GCC countries have similar political and economic systems and, therefore, mutual cooperation will be fruitful and problem-free when fear of Saudi domination has been eliminated. If American intervention will give them reassurance and consolidate mutual trust between the US and GCC countries, it will be an achievement comparable to what has been done for ASEAN countries.

Iran is comparable to China, with its equally long history of civilization and past history of independent and proud empire. If it is allowed to exist and is to be accommodated in the world community, it will be one of the most reliable bastions against Soviet influence, just like present-day China. What should be avoided, however, is the disruption of an Iranian national entity and confrontation between the U.S. and Iran, two events that would create ample opportunities for the Soviet Union to expand its influence in the region.

The dispatch of the American fleet to the gulf is a good and necessary action as long as it is requested and supported by the gulf nations. Future American action should be conducted under the principle of continuous military and political coordination with the gulf nations so that American presence will always be welcomed and supported by them. In addition, American action should avoid confrontation with Iran. Limited Iranian provocations should not be answered by escalation. Thus, the U.S. can convey to Iran its will for a political settlement.

On an arms embargo, the military balance on the Iran-Iraq front is not at all unfavorable for Iraq. Of course, the situation changes in case of a collapse of morale on one of the two sides. In that case any intervention, short of direct military participation, will have very little effect. The effect of an arms embargo on the war will be less than the effect of the American blockade of Haiphong Harbor in Vietnam by mines and would not change the course of the war.

International sanctions by the Security Council may not be avoided when urged by the gulf nations, as it serves as a reassurance to them. It is dangerous and unnecessary, however, to escalate tensions to the point of confrontation. Confrontation would limit the freedom of future American diplomacy, inevitably establishing an image of Iran, in the process of the escalation of confrontation, among the American public as an outlaw in the international community and an enemy of the United States that should be destroyed by all means. In this connection it is a matter of concern that current American policy is being formed partly by the rancor deriving from memories of the hostage incident and massacres of U.S. marines in Beirut. It is again embarrassing that the only force that checks and balances this sentiment is noninterventionism, one of the Vietnam syndromes. American policy should be based on a long-term strategy on the Middle East, reserving a flexibility for future actions.

Whatever the course of the war may be, it is always in America's best interest, while firmly reassuring the security of the gulf nations, to reserve the chance of a political settlement with Iran.

A European Perspective

Dominique Moîsi

This paper was prepared for presentation at a March 1988 Study Group. It has not been revised to reflect the cease-fire that has taken effect in the Persian Gulf war.

In the late 1970s a common European position effectively existed in the Middle East. As a result of the oil shock, of Israel's increasingly powerful and isolated profile that was slowly undermining Europe's emotional memories and guilt, Europe was able to find a common position and to present a "third way," thanks largely to the competitive pressures of France and Great Britain. Its best and most ambitious formulation was the Venice declaration of June 1980. It could be said that in the manner of a Greek chorus the Europeans commented on events rather than shaped them. This formulation of a distinct European position was not welcomed by the United States. For many Americans Europe was "stooping for oil," and its policy in the Middle East was a "perfect symbol of her decadence and cowardice, a foreign policy based on economics and governed by fear."

Today, on the contrary, Europe's collective muscle-flexing in the gulf—and the presence of a sizable European armada— is largely seen as a "quiet plus" for the West and is most welcome by the American administration. In its attempts to justify domestically the American presence in front of mounting congressional criticisms, the U.S. can point to the fact that it is not alone in the effort.

But in spite of the presence of nearly forty European ships in the Gulf War Zone, of close cooperation among them, and very probably with the U.S. Navy (maybe more than anyone is saying publicly), can one speak of a common European posture in the gulf? When it comes to the war between Iran and Iraq, do European positions, in spite of the various U.N. Security Council's resolutions, present an ostensible unity of facade that any rapid and brutal escalation in the gulf war affecting Western fleets would dramatically unravel?

Can one even use the term "Europe" in the gulf? What are the unified or different European positions on the Iran-Iraq war and on the freedom of circulation in the gulf zone? How do the Europeans view the respective role of the two superpowers, the United States and the Soviet Union, and the role of that newcomer, Japan?

In this presentation of Europe's position, I feel I am at a great disadvantage compared with my two distinguished colleagues and friends, for Europe, unlike the United States and Japan, is not yet—and may never be—a political reality. Also, as a Frenchman, I will give you a European perspective that is not, I fear, totally objective and distanced.

The European Role in the Gulf

To speak of Europe in the gulf is an overstatement of sorts. Only two countries stand out from the pack as having a global, political, military, and economic role in the region: Great Britain and France, and these two countries are engaged in a competitive partnership that sometimes evokes the memory of a mini-Fashoda, divided as they are by a common history and conflicting policies. A third country, Italy, has a significant military and economic presence, but its diplomatic role, berated for so long by itself, is much more discreet. Italy's involvement is also the object of strong domestic debates, despite its recent willingness to translate economic successes and a relative political stability into a more assertive diplomacy. The Federal Republic of Germany, in spite of the fact that for the first time it has sent four warships to NATO in the Mediterranean to take over duties of Allied vessels diverted to the gulf from the western Mediterranean has mainly kept an economic role. As for the Netherlands and Belgium, their combined force of four minesweepers and a

minesweeper command and support ship has represented
more a symbol of Allied solidarity than a decisive contribution to the security of the region, and their global influence is,
to use an understatement, limited.

To a large extent, therefore, any study of a European role in
the gulf must begin (and probably end) with a comparative
assessment of British and French policies. Great Britain's
junior partner as a colonial power in the Middle East, France,
was by and large historically absent from the gulf area. Such
an "historical virginity" is often advanced by the French to
justify a more accepted role. The region was essentially under
British control, and if this constitutes a basis for better
understanding if not influence, it is also a source of resent-
ment. A similar argument was used even further by the
Japanese themselves when, in the wake of the U.S. hostage
crisis in Iran, they tried to take over the U.S. role in commerce,
by claiming that, at least, they were not former imperial
colonial powers in that part of the world and that they should
be accepted as a new kind of go-between linking the
industrial North and the developing South.

France's and Great Britain's goals may be presented in the
same manner: First, bringing an end to the war between Iran
and Iraq by working at present for the implementation of the
Security Council's Resolution 598, which provides for a cease-
fire and negotiated settlement. And, second, by upholding the
principle of freedom of navigation through the maintenance
of a naval presence. But France and Great Britain are, in fact,
separated in their gulf policies by history, diplomatic styles,
competitive economic realities (especially as far as arms sales
are concerned), and differing political choices.

Great Britain, since its withdrawal east of Aden in 1969, has
kept a low visibility in that part of the world—with the
exception of the Sultanate of Oman—coupled with a discreet
but nonnegligible influence. Such an approach has led Great
Britain to adhere to a policy of strict neutrality in the Iran-
Iraq war, a position encouraged by its perception of Iran as the
key geopolitical actor in the long-run and by the difficult
burden of its colonial past with Iraq. British neutrality was

also facilitated by the relative "benign neglect" toward oil, which the North Sea resources allowed it to maintain.

For France, this British neutrality was, in fact, perceived as being tilted much too favorably toward Iran, a preference illustrated by Great Britain's willingness to place on the same footing when it came to an arms embargo Iraq, the country willing to adhere to U.N. resolutions and Iran, the country bent on exporting its revolution. In the minds of the French, an arms embargo equally applied to the two countries could only constitute a severe blow to Iraq, given the inequality of their respective situations. Iraq relies on "official sources of weapons"—including France, while Iran has benefited and would continue to do so from the "gray markets" of the underworld of arms sales.

If Great Britain has been keen on maintaining a strict neutrality, followed on that line by the Germans and the Italians who like the Japanese themselves have maintained large economic contacts with Iran (Italy is taking care of French diplomatic interests in Teheran), the French attitude has been characterized by one of clear support for the Iraqi position, which recent events have not seriously affected.

French policy in the gulf is based on three principles:

- There should not be a victorious or a defeated power.
- France should not lose contact with the majority trend within the Security Council of the United Nations and, in particular, among the five great powers.
- The need to respect our previous international contracts.

To abide by these principles, France had to pursue two goals: to prevent an Iraqi defeat and to promote the reestablishment of peace. If France is more involved in Iraq today, it is because of its past involvement in the beginning of the 70s. At that time, France wanted to widen the scope of its Arab policy, until then limited to countries such as Syria, Lebanon, and Egypt, with which France had traditional relations. With Iraq, France was setting foot in a region that had been hitherto largely dominated by the Anglo-Saxon influence.

France's rapprochement with Iraq in the early 1970s was intended to secure oil supplies and profitable markets. It also had the political advantage of fostering a unique Western presence in a country that had become too dependent on the Soviet Union. The elegant Kissingerian division of labor between the French in Baghdad and the Americans in Teheran did not survive the fall of the Shah in 1978 and the ensuing military ambitions of Iraqi President Saddam Hussein.

In comparison, Franco-Iranian relations on the eve of the war were much less developed in spite of the influence of French culture and French language within the Iranian elite. Unlike Great Britain, the Federal Republic, or Japan, France had not been able to benefit from the boom of the Iranian economy.

Moreover, France had started a very ambitious program of arms sales to Iraq, materialized by important contracts that turned Iraq, until 1982 and the beginning of the Iraqi financial difficulties, into the first customer of France in the field of armaments, even before Saudi Arabia.

French military support of Iraq represents approximately 10 percent of Iraqi military needs compared with the 80 percent provided by the Soviet Union. But it is a highly visible and highly sophisticated support concentrated on air defense and air force. In fact, France's support of Iraq, beyond its financial or military dimension, has been mainly political since France, despite its recent attempt to normalize its relations with Iran, has never jeopardized or drastically modified its relations with Iraq.

France's support of Iraq can also be explained by an ideological element. The religious dimension of the new Iranian regime after the elimination of Bakhtiar or Bani Sadr have imposed the image of Iran as a cruel, irrational and reactionary country (which does not mean that Iraq should be perceived as a democratic and gentle regime).

But the militant proselytism of Islamic fundamentalism in Iran could only threaten the Arab policy of France and even be perceived by the French as a new indirect threat: two million Muslims are living in France and France's relations with Maghreb are crucially important.

If France's policy toward the conflict has been different from that of Great Britain and globally the rest of Europe, it has not only been in terms of content but also in terms of style. For West Germany, Italy, and one could even say Britain—with the exception of the Falklands War—the principal foreign policy objective seems to have been to shelter the country from the heavy clouds of the international arena. For France, instead, a highly visible foreign policy has been a way of establishing the nation's international presence.

A policy designed to provide security in energy led, by a series of unwanted steps, to a situation of physical insecurity first for French forces in Lebanon, then for French nationals taken hostage in Lebanon, and then for French citizens on French soil, as forces in the Middle East were trying to punish France for its global Middle Eastern policy from Lebanon to the gulf war and impose a new Middle Eastern policy on it.

The symbol of a hated West in a region of turmoil, identity crisis, and war, France, unfortunately for it, combined a mixture of high visibility and high vulnerability. A policy of ambiguous leniency under President Giscard d'Estaing had encouraged the impression that France would prove less resolute in its determination to fight terrorism. Such a policy was followed by a confusing reorganization of the French secret services under François Mitterrand. The French became highly exposed in the Middle East, just at the time when their secret services were the least prepared to handle the challenge of hostages in Lebanon and terrorists in Paris. Because of its past choices in a region that used to be a former sphere of influence—shared on a junior footing with Great Britain— France tried to limit the cost of its ambitions. First and foremost, it attempted to restore a more balanced position between Iran and Iraq. Normalization with Iran, long overdue and attempted with dynamism if not clarity by Foreign Minister Roland Dumas, was deemed to be essential diplomatically, and even justified on domestic grounds. Prime Minister Chirac, once he arrived in Matignon, was initially convinced that to get the French hostages back would constitute a plus in the eyes of public opinion. The high cost, given rising Iranian demands and the slow path of such a difficult balancing exercise (France wanted to normalize with Iran without ceasing to send weapons to Iraq), proved to be an impossible task. The revelations of the Irangate scandal, linked to the growing awareness by the French authorities that French public opinion was in favor of a policy of firmness, led at first to a de facto abandonment of the attempt to normalize relations with Iran, then to a worsening of relations, and finally to reescalation of provocations that led to the breakdown of diplomatic relations in the summer of 1987.

The consequences of the process of cohabitation on France's Middle Eastern policy are difficult to assess. The competitive partnership between the presidency and the prime minister's office and its concrete manifestation, the foreign ministry, were to a large extent transcended by the key role played by the ministry of the interior, whose power of initiative stemmed from the predominance of the actions against terrorism. Moreover, Mitterrand's vision and Chirac's priorities were largely compatible. Both leaders, for instance, had been in agreement in their refusal to allow American planes to fly over France during the raid over Libya in April 1986. A strong sense of national independence and a refusal to permit what would have been perceived in Paris as subordination to a foreign will united the two men. More specifically, Chirac's longstanding relationship with Iraq and the Arab world could well fit with Mitterrand's strong rejection of an Islamic fundamentalism incarnated by Iran's mullahs. Such a congruence of views did not suppress the fact that the duality of the executive was certainly used and will still be used by France's adversaries to manipulate it politically and to reap more profits.

But France's problems in the Middle East go well beyond cohabitation. They stem from a lack of modesty, balance, and firmness and from the fact, ultimately, that the Middle East is not Francophone Africa—France's last sphere of influence in the world. The stakes are much higher and the military means involved are incomparable. How could France not seem bogged down in the Middle East when the superpowers themselves are increasingly aware of their limited capabilities? It was in Lebanon that the contradictions between French ambitions and capabilities proved most devastating. Behind the continuation of a traditional and ritualized call for a renewed role of France in the diplomatic process in the Israeli-Palestinian conflict, or in Lebanon, Mitterrand and Chirac want, in fact, to minimize France's vulnerability in the Middle East without forfeiting their own sense of honor, dignity, and the appearance of maintaining a traditional policy of presence linked to France's history and culture. But in spite of the French vessels patrolling the gulf, the relation between France's deeds and France's words in the Middle East appears increasingly artificial.

How can one assess the role that the Europeans are playing in the gulf zone? The military cooperation provided by the Europeans has proven very useful to the United States, offering the Americans military help without any constraint on their freedom of action and none of the financial responsibility or political risks that an integrated force would entail. The implications for future military cooperation among European nations and with the United States of the gulf deployment may prove important in the future. Loose coordination rather than an integrated command may offer greater military efficiency and ease political frictions among NATO allies when they confront threats to Western security outside the NATO area. In the past, the U.S. administration had suspected that a nonintegrated approach would leave the military burden to the United States, allowing the European allies to confine their role to quiet diplomacy. In recent months, the Americans seem to have accepted European reservations on integrated efforts. The European argument, defended with special energy by France, seems to have prevailed. The less integrated the reassurance is, the more acceptable it is for the gulf states and, therefore, the more credible it will become. If the West is perceived as the enemy, why emphasize the Western dimension by any institutional attempt to present European and American efforts in a unified way? In the gulf, naval cooperation among the various Western nations has proven that quiet coordination can work.

There is another dimension of the European role that, given its nature, can only be mentioned but that has proven very useful. In matters of internal security, European countries, France and the Federal Republic of Germany in particular, have contributed significantly to the training of the police and counterterrorist forces of countries such as Saudi Arabia.

Ultimately, the European role in the gulf has proved not only useful, if only marginally, to the gulf security but also important for the harmony of the Atlantic Alliance at a crucial time in the East-West dialogue. It has also represented for Europe itself, in spite of its divisions, a symbol of its potential future unity, and institutionally it has reinforced the Western European Union (WEU), which has been used as a convenient non-NATO umbrella to coordinate European efforts.

The Europeans and the Superpowers

What has been the European perception of the role of the superpowers in the gulf?

To a large extent, the role of the United States in the Middle East and the gulf has traditionally been seen with a degree of irritation and criticism. A newcomer and a geographically distant actor in the region, the United States had nevertheless managed to be the strongest partner. It had placed the Soviet Union in the inferior position of having to constantly catch up, thanks to powerful economic means and a capacity to project military force. With access to military bases and a powerful Sixth Fleet, the United States had been able to balance the Soviet advantage of geographic proximity. But its "nouveau riche" behavior did not prevent the U.S.'s biggest failure until today: the collapse of Iran, the country it had selected to be the regional pillar of stability in the gulf. In the late 70s, in the wake of the Iranian revolution, the Europeans thought they could "educate" the United States.

For them, the U.S. had failed in Iran on two counts. A prisoner of its own modernization model, badly informed by certain experts in the social sciences when the advice of historians and anthropologists would have been more preferable, the United States had been incapable of understanding the religious culture and the economic and social problems the government of the Shah had to confront, an insensitivity symbolic of American failure elsewhere. The Europeans felt they were better equipped than the United States to understand the nature of a revolutionary process and the culture and religion of these societies. Their own history—the French revolution in particular—and their traditional presence in the region, commercial at first and then colonial, had made them more responsive to local opinions. In abandoning its most faithful ally, the Shah, with an inconsistency that was equalled only by the massive support it had previously given him, the United States had also raised doubts about its credibility elsewhere. Such doubts were reinforced by the tragic failure in 1983 of the multinational force in Lebanon, whose mandate was at least ambiguous.

The Irangate crisis could only reinforce an old and negative image of the United States, all the more preoccupying because it coincided in Europe with a new and more positive image of the Soviet Union under an energetic leader who was beating Ronald Reagan at his own game of public relations. Coming so soon after Reykjavik, which was seen in Europe as a daring and unprepared diplomatic venture, Irangate could only confirm European apprehensions. Not only were the Americans unpredictable, amateurish, and adventurist, but their diplomacy was unreliable and incompetent. The arms sales to Iran raised a fundamental question: was American foreign policy destined to fail because it was the product of one of the most complex democratic systems in the world? The intricate checks and balances between the executive branch and Congress and the sophisticated suicidal games within the executive seemed to fit at best an isolationist United States. These games did not correspond to the foreign policy needs of the world's leading power. The Iran-Contra hearings of last summer could only confirm European worries and puzzlement.

Today, nine months after the decision to put Kuwaiti tankers under the American flag and six months since the deployment of the fleet to escort them, America's image in the gulf and American Middle Eastern policy seem to be producing a reversal of perceptions. Europeans who were initially skeptical are now much more positive in their assessment of U.S. policy. American policy has been crucial in the rebuilding of the gulf Arab states' confidence that they are not alone in defending themselves against Iran. The United States seems to be defending at long last the states' territorial integrity and political independence. The United States has gained the right of landing planes in case of emergencies at Saudi airports, and they can use their AWACS planes to keep an eye on the Arab emirates. The American commitments have reduced Iran's military options and may have increased the pressure on Iran to give up its war effort against Iraq. One senses in Teheran a growing feeling of frustration toward the continuation of the conflict. The price of this new restraint on Iran's actions may have been to redirect Teheran's efforts from military activities in the classical sense to other forms of violence, terrorism in particular.

The United States' political efforts at the United Nations have also increased Iran's diplomatic isolation and probably the difficulty and expenses that Teheran encounters in acquiring arms. More basically, the lesson to be derived from the American presence in the gulf is that the United States after Vietnam can still use its military strength to support a political strategy. United States performance in the gulf is helping to restore confidence that it has the will to decide on a course and to abide by it. Yet, a number of questions remain unresolved. In its policy in the gulf, the United States had set itself three goals:

- To preserve the freedom of navigation.
- To reassure its allies, the moderate conservative regimes.

• To keep the Soviet Union at a distance.

This third objective has not been achieved; quite the opposite. In fact, one could say that the primary beneficiary of the "internationalization" of the conflict is the Soviet Union, which has gained a seat as an "interested party" in a zone where it had traditionally been marginal. In the future, the U.S. administration will be confronted with difficult dilemmas: How to convince Congress to maintain a substantial military presence if there is an escalation in the gulf or even an accidental attack against the U.S. fleet; How to reassure the moderate Arab regimes without pushing Iran into the arms of the Soviet Union; How to stop the war without seeing a brutal collapse of oil prices linked to the overproduction of the two former belligerents, now attempting to rebuild their economies.

The Soviet Role in the Gulf

Contrary to the United States, European countries, even if they want to keep the Soviet Union at bay in the Middle East and the gulf at large, recognize the legitimacy of its involvement there. In the Middle East, the key question for the future is not whether to integrate the Soviet Union but when to do so. To bring the Soviet Union in too early in any peace process is to give them a diplomatic reward that may be used by Moscow to exercise diplomatic pressures for its own interests. Yet, the Western dilemma is uneasy: how and when to integrate a great power whose rules of the game are not the same as the West's, whose goals are ultimately antithetical to the West's—since stability can be for the Soviet Union only a temporary objective—but whose absence will ensure that it will try to unsettle what has been achieved without it, if indeed any differences can ever be settled at all without its participation.

The Soviet Union's main advantages in the Middle East have always been twofold: first, its geographic proximity and a long-standing involvement in the region (if not in the gulf) allow it to legitimize its ambitions in historical terms. The Soviet Union, thanks to a common border with Turkey, Iran, and Afghanistan, can claim the same regional interest in the Middle East as the United States in Central America. Second, a long-term ideological vision gives Moscow the possibility of presenting itself alternatively as a status quo or as a revolutionary power bent on modifying the existing Middle Eastern order. The Soviets, as faithful inheritors of the Czars, fear an "undue" Western presence in the region. In their quest for parity with the United States, they are also looking for a recognition of their superpower status in the region: they want to have client states and they do not want to be excluded from any peacemaking formula for symbolic as well as for objective reasons. A land of opportunity, the Middle East has also grown to be increasingly a land of vulnerability for the Soviet Union. The rise of Islamic fundamentalism, especially after the Iranian revolution and the Soviet invasion of Afghanistan, appears increasingly to be a major concern for the Soviets. With a Muslim majority constituting 20 percent of the Soviet population, the Soviet Union can only be worried by the growing hostility to atheistic communism and the heightened self-confidence of the Islamic minorities within the Soviet landmass.

Iran presents a special problem for the Soviet Union. Initially encouraged by the fall of the Shah, it had hoped to build a special relationship with Iran that should have outweighed in Soviet minds the danger of Khomeiniism. Under Gorbachev, the Soviet Union has demonstrated a greater dynamism in its diplomatic activity in the Middle East, improving its relations with Oman, the United Arab Emirates, Bahrain, Kuwait, North Yemen, Jordan, and Egypt as well as an attempt at better relations with Saudi Arabia.

The Soviet Union's recent diplomatic maneuvering with Israel reflects its willingness to dramatize its new policy of *glasnost* with the West under Gorbachev. It may also translate the fact that the Soviet Union feels more confident today that the Soviet-Arab relations are strong enough to survive such a test.

Also, while clearly not wishing to see the defeat of its ally, Iraq, and at odds with Iran on a range of regional and ideological issues, Moscow has maintained correct relations with Iran and positioned itself for the possible adoption of a mediating role between the two belligerents.

In addition, the Soviet Union may become more eager than any other country to see the conflict end, in light of the regional gains made by the United States and its allies since the reflagging began.

Japan, and the International Efforts to End the War

As far as Japan is concerned, its role in the gulf war is seen by many in the West and especially in France, as opportunistic and too tilted toward Iran.

If the Japanese perceive themselves as "in the middle," if they believe they are acting in the global interest of the West by keeping the doors open to Iran and if they deny the mercantile nature of their policy, they do so in a rather defensive manner and are unable to fully convince their Western partners.

For the Japanese, some kind of division of labor exists in the gulf between the Americans, who are bent on preserving Arab moderate states, and the Japanese, who are trying to preserve Iran in the long run as a stable country, open to the West and not under the Soviet flag.

Beyond the argument, what is at stake is the ability of the Japanese to play a global diplomatic role.

From the Japanese point of view, the Middle East and the gulf have the direct advantage of being important for them and far from the Asian scene, where the legacy of the past is still looming large. More fundamentally, the question is: for the West, the Japanese are Asian and should take greater responsibilities in Asia to alleviate the U.S. burden. As for the

Japanese, they perceive themselves as Westerners and clearly not as Asians, a perception shared by Asians who see them as Japanese and therefore different. Japan's diplomatic dilemma is of a dual nature. On the one hand, it will have to return to being a political animal: if the United States has more commitments than means, the reverse is true of Japan. On the other hand, Japan finds it difficult to define a role for itself that would appear as independent, yet useful for the international community and not negative for its image. Its involvement in the gulf war translates into its difficult attempt to answer that fundamental dilemma.

As the conflict has decisively entered a new phase with an internationalization of the war and a sudden sharpening of international interest in ending the war, the key interrogations revolve around Iran.

Iran is now under heavy political pressure. Its freedom to maneuver in the gulf is constrained. It faces the possibility of international sanctions, possibly in the form of a mandatory global arms embargo. What are the Iranian government's real intentions? What should the international community do about them? If the Iranians are really war-weary and are seeking an end to the war, could a sign of willingness on the part of the Security Council to name Iraq as the original aggressor in the conflict open the way for a true dialogue with Iran? Is the Islamic Republic—convinced that time is on its side—simply buying time and playing with the United Nations?

In confronting Teheran, given our real ignorance of what is going on within its fractious leadership, one should combine a mixture of inducement and coercion. Iran is clearly a revolutionary regime intent on exporting its revolution or subverting its neighbors. But it is also a key geostrategic actor that can display a remarkable pragmatism in its diplomacy, as exemplified by its cooperation with Saudi Arabia in OPEC to support oil prices. The objectives of the Western powers should be to induce Iran and Iraq to wind down hostilities to a more limited level. The prolongation of the Western naval presence in the gulf is a key element of that strategy. As the war in the gulf continues to escalate to new levels of horror, one can seriously wonder whether the two countries would have resorted to nuclear weapons if they had possessed them. This interrogation raises once more the issue of nuclear proliferation in the Third World, and one that the recent sales of Chinese missiles to Saudi Arabia can only underscore.

APPENDIX
Text of U.N. Security Council Resolution 598

THE SECURITY COUNCIL,

REAFFIRMING its Resolution 585 (1986),

DEEPLY CONCERNED that, despite its calls for a cease-fire, the conflict, the conflict between Iran and Iraq continues unabated, with further heavy loss of human life and material destruction,

DEPLORING the initiation and continuation of the conflict,

DEPLORING also the bombing of purely civilian population centers, attacks on neutral shipping or civilian aircraft, the violation of international humanitarian law and other laws of armed conflict, and in particular, the use of chemical weapons contrary to obligations under the 1925 Geneva Protocol,

DEEPLY CONCERNED that further escalation and widening of the conflict may take place,

DETERMINED to bring to an end all military actions between Iran and Iraq,

CONVINCED that a comprehensive, just, honorable and durable settlement should be achieved between Iran and Iraq,

RECALLING the provisions of the Charter of the United Nations, and in particular the obligation of all member states to settle their international disputes by peaceful means in such a manner that international peace and security and justice are not endangered,

DETERMINING that there exists a breach of the peace as regards the conflict between Iran and Iraq,

ACTING under Articles 39 and 40 of the Charter of the United Nations,

1. DEMANDS that, as a first step towards a negotiated settlement, Iran and Iraq observe an immediate cease-fire, discontinue all military actions on land, at sea and in the air, and withdraw all forces to the internationally recognized boundaries without delay;

2. REQUESTS the Secretary General to dispatch a team of United Nations observers to verify, confirm and supervise the cease-fire and withdrawal and further requests the Secretary General to make the necessary arrangements in consultation with the parties and to submit a report thereon to the Security Council;

3. URGES that prisoners of war be released and repatriated without delay after the cessation of active hostilities in accordance with the Third Geneva Convention of 12 August 1949;

4. CALLS UPON Iran and Iraq to cooperate with the Secretary General in implementing this resolution and in mediation efforts to achieve a comprehensive, just and honorable settlement, acceptable to both sides, of all outstanding issues, in accordance with the principles contained in the Charter of the United Nations;

5. CALLS UPON all other states to exercise the utmost restraint and to refrain from any act which may lead to further escalation and widening of the conflict, and thus to facilitate the implementation of the present resolution;

6. REQUESTS the Secretary General to explore, in consultation with Iran and Iraq, the question of entrusting an impartial body with inquiring into responsibility for the conflict and to report to the Security Council as soon as possible;

7. RECOGNIZES the magnitude of the damage inflicted during the conflict and the need for reconstruction efforts, with appropriate international assistance, once the conflict is ended and, in this regard, requests the Secretary General to assign a team of experts to study the question of reconstruction and to report to the Security Council;

8. FURTHER REQUESTS the S.G. to examine, in consultation with Iran and Iraq and with other states of the region, measures to enhance the security and stability of the region;

9. REQUESTS the Secretary General to keep the Security Council informed on the implementation of this resolution;

10. DECIDES to meet again as necessary to consider further steps to ensure compliance with this resolution.

Council on Foreign Relations
Study Group on Great Power Interests in the Persian Gulf/Arabian Sea

James R. Schlesinger, Chairman, Center for Strategic and International Studies
Paul Jabber, Group Director, Council on Foreign Relations
Eleanor Tejirian, Rapporteur, Columbia University

Discussion Leaders

Dominique Moîsi, French Institute for International Relations
Hisahiko Okazaki, Japan's Ambassador to Saudi Arabia
Gary Sick, Columbia University

James Akins, Consultant
Kenneth J. Bialkin, Willkie, Farr & Gallagher
Ainslie Embree, Columbia University
William Gleysteen, Jr., Council on Foreign Relations
Ted Greenwood, Columbia University
Peter Grose, *Foreign Affairs*
Judith Gustafson, Council on Foreign Relations
Thor Hanson, Vice Adm. USN (Ret.)
Selig Harrison, Carnegie Endowment for International Peace
Karen Elliot House, *The Wall Street Journal*
Geoffrey Kemp, Carnegie Endowment for International Peace
Zalmay Khalilzad, Department of State
Judith Kipper, Brookings Institution
Stanley Kwieciak, Jr. Col. USA, Visiting Military Fellow, Council on Foreign Relations
Richard Lawrence, Lt. Gen. USA
Walter J. Levy, W. J. Levy Consultant Corp.
Paul Lewis, *The New York Times*

John Lichtblau, Petroleum Industry Research Foundation
Michael Mandelbaum, Council on Foreign Relations
Eric Margolis, *Toronto Sun*
Thomas McHale, Drexel Burnham Lambert
Warren Nelson, House Armed Services Committee
Margaret Osmer-McQuade, Council on Foreign Relations
Gerald Pollack, Overseas Shipping Group
Alan Romberg, Council on Foreign Relations
Arthur Ross, Central National-Gottesman, Inc.
Dankwart Rustow, New York University
Nadav Safran, Harvard University
Howard M. Squadron, Squadron, Ellenoff, Plesent & Lehrer
Michael Sterner, The IRC Group
Alan Stoga, Kissinger Associates
Jack Sunderland, President, Oil Company
John Temple Swing, Council on Foreign Relations
Phillips Talbot, Asia Society
Peter Tarnoff, Council on Foreign Relations
Bernard Trainor, *The New York Times*
Stansfield Turner, Adm. USN (Ret.)

Guests

Hisako Shimura, United Nations
Wang Junmei, PRC Embassy, Washington
Alexei Podtserob, USSR Mission to the UN

This Study Group was underwritten by Arthur Ross

About the Authors

Paul Jabber has headed the Council's Middle East Program since 1985, and recently rejoined Bankers Trust Co. of New York as Vice President for Middle East Merchant Banking. In 1975-82, he taught in the Political Science Department at the University of California, Los Angeles. He is the author of *Israel and Nuclear Weapons* (1971) and *Not By War Alone: Security and Arms Control in the Middle East* (1982).

Gary Sick recently left as deputy director of the International Affairs program of the Ford Foundation to devote himself to full-time writing. He served on the Middle East staff of the National Security Council during the Ford, Carter, and early Reagan administrations. After a career of twenty-four years in the U.S. Navy, he left active duty in 1981 with the rank of Captain. He is the author of *All Fall Down: America's Tragic Encounter with Iran* (1985).

Hisahiko Okazaki, a career diplomat in Japan's foreign service, recently completed a tour of duty as ambassador to the Kingdom of Saudi Arabia. In 1978-81 he was attached as Councillor to Japan's Self-Defense Agency, and in 1982-84 served as Director General of Information, Analysis, Research and Planning at the Ministry of Foreign Affairs. He has written several books and articles, including *A Grand Strategy for Japanese Defense* (1986).

Dominique Moïsi is associate director of the French Institute of International Relations (IFRI), and chief editor of the quarterly *Politique Etrangere*. He teaches international relations at the University of Paris and is a regular contributor for the *International Herald Tribune* and *Los Angeles Times*. He has published extensively on French foreign policy and Middle East affairs.